The original building c. 1840

Cork 2005
European Capital of Culture

James Bourne painted by James Brennan (R.H.A.) around 1850. James Brennan was head of the School of Design and was an excellent teacher and artist. "His homely pictures, painted during holiday time in Inchigeela, were faithful in representation and sympathetic in treatment" R.H.A Society Vol XLVIII (1943)

The Story of
WOODFORD BOURNE

WINE IMPORTERS ESTAB.^D 1750

David Nicholson

with

Philip Mackeown

Acknowledgements

In preparing this book, I received help and encouragement from very many people without whom this project would not have been possible and whose help I would like to acknowledge here.

Ken Peare and Fiona O'Connor at Woodford Bourne , for their support for the project from original idea to launch. Jerry Cashman, Terry Connolly, Hugh Hall, Gordon Hunter and Tim O'Sullivan for their enthusiasm in the preparation of the launch and promotion of the book.

I would particularly like to acknowledge those former employees of the company who lent photographs and gave of their time in reminiscing about the history of the business.

Bob Berwyn, John James, Raymond Jones, Margaret Larmonie, Mahon Lee, The O'Morchoe and Ronnie Payne for reading and commenting so constructively, on earlier drafts of the book.

In addition Pamela Bradley, Roger Hall, Peter Morehead, John Roche and Helen Sheehy for advice and support as the project developed.

Tim Cadogan of the Cork County Library and Brian McGinn of the Cork Archives Institute for assisting me in the early stages of the research into the company, its origins and roots in Cork city.

Tom Doorley and Declan Hassett for their assistance at the later stages of the preparation of the book and their advice on the final edition.

Finally, I would like to thank Robert Merrick and Michael O'Grady and the team at Bandon Printers for their patience in the design, laying out and production of the story of the company.

David Nicholson.

David Nicholson
August, 2005

Editor & Publisher 2005   W.B. Publications,
            Diamond Lodge, Monkstown, Co. Cork, Ireland.
            Tel/Fax: +353 21 4842160 Email: davidnic@eircom.net

Photography   John Roche Photography

Print   Bandon Printers

ISBN-10 0-9551206-0-8 ISBN-13 978-0-9551206-0-2

Contents

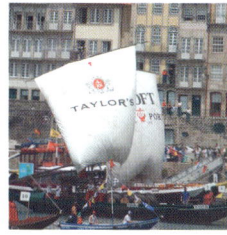

Foreword

As the fourth and last generation of the Nicholson family to work in the wine business I have felt a genuine sense of responsibility. The story of the foundation and subsequent fortunes of this well known and long established grocery and wine company had to be recorded for posterity.

Covering 250 years of the history of Woodford Bourne, and at the same time tracing the Nicholson family's involvement proved a challenging and not surprisingly, time consuming task. In doing so I have had the valuable assistance of Philip Mackeown and together we hope that we have made the story of Woodford Bourne an enjoyable and informative read.

The company experienced changing economic fortunes, changes in consumer tastes, the introduction of supermarkets and later the developing popularity of wine as a social drink, all set against the backdrop of the ever changing political and social landscape in Ireland. Meeting these challenges required constant innovation and new ventures of which it has been possible only to touch on the main ones in this history. The rejuvenation and expansion of the table wine trade of the twentieth century occurred during my working lifetime. I was partly responsible for this, so not surprisingly, telling its story has brought back many happy memories. Unquestionably Woodford Bourne was one of the forerunners in maturing the taste-buds of the increasingly affluent Irish people, successfully responding to this evolution with the sourcing of new and varied wines from all parts of the world.

The story of Woodford Bourne would not be complete without the acknowledgement of the many suppliers, customers and business associates who put their trust in the company over so many years. Their contribution, and the lasting relationships build up with Woodford Bourne, enabled the company to consistently strive for excellence and efficiency of service and value.

Woodford Bourne was a happy place to work. For many employees this was their only job and their loyalty, commitment and enthusiasm fostered a strong team effort. The family and I would like to recognise the efforts of hundreds of dedicated and able employees throughout the organisation, without whom nothing would have been achieved. As a representative of the Nicholson family I am proud of what was achieved and the success that many staff members went on to make of their own businesses.

As an added interest, many illustrations have been included: copies of original labels, Christmas lists, photographs of the original cellars, Royal Warrants as well as photographs or portraits of the Nicholson family. Fortunately, many of the old records of the company had been preserved often turning up in the unlikeliest of places. These have been used fully by us and include: Bulk Wine Imports since 1871, Register of Coffee and Tea Imports since 1890, Minutes of Board Meetings since 1905, Letters, Reports and Accounts. Upon completion of the project, these are to be donated to the Boole Library, University College Cork, where they will form part of the archive of historical documents.

On a final note I would hope that you enjoy this story which is meant to capture the essence of a much loved family business. Although the wholesale business was sold some time ago, and continues to thrive, parts of the original business still remain under the direct ownership and management of the Nicholson family.

For me, writing this book completes my commitment to what has been a very enjoyable and important part of my life. Finally, I would like to dedicate this book to my wife, Joan, whose calm understanding has provided much support to a very preoccupied editor and co-editor, over the last two years.

David Nicholson
August 2005

A Note on Terminology

Writing the story of a company with such a long span of history, inevitably raises the issue of currency representation and conversion. Where the "£" symbol is used, it refers to both Irish Pound and UK sterling amounts up to March 1979. Following the split from sterling, all amounts thereafter are in Irish Pounds, or Punts, and are denominated by the sign "IR£". Following the introduction of the Euro in 2000, all amounts are given in Euros.

Throughout the story I have attempted to indicate the approximate value of the historical currency amount, in present day (2005) Euro terms. I hope, in so doing, to give the reader an insight into the scale of the investments, sales and profits, which were considerable relative to the commercial landscape of the time.

Philip Mackeown
August 2005

CHAPTER 1

The Origins of the Company

"Smell the Coffee, Taste the Wine"

French wine was already "making glad the heart of men" and women in Ireland in the eighteenth century. Shipments of Bordeaux wine were sizeable, prompting a visitor to note: "The rather dour Lord Chesterfield, commenting on the then current scene observed that ' one gentleman in ten in Ireland is impoverished by the great quantity of claret which for mistaken notions of hospitality and dignity, they think it necessary should be drunk in their houses' and that the 'affectation of drinking wine has even got into the middle and lower ranks of the people'" *T.P Whelehan p.2.*

Into this setting came the Maziere family, Huguenot émigrés from the former Province of Aunis north of Saintonge in the Charente-Maritime region of France. They settled in Cork and Dublin in the early part of the eighteenth century and in 1750 set up a wine, spirits and beer business in Falconer's Lane in Cork City.

Peter Maziere commenced the bottling of porter in Falconer's Lane which runs parallel to Academy Street in the centre of Cork between Patrick's Street and Nelson (later Emmet) Place. The business was also developed with the importing of brandy, marsala and port wine from France, Sicily and Portugal. He also undertook the brewing of porter which was widely consumed at the time. He was a freeman of Cork City and one of the original proprietors of the Cork Institution. He was also involved in further commercial ventures of a maritime nature being a proprietor of the St George Steam Packet Company and the owner of the Superb steamship which travelled between Cork and Bristol.

Peter Maziere featured in the journal of a certain Mr Samuel Reilly on the occasion of their imprisonment by supporters of Wolfe Tone on their way from Cork to Dublin, in 1798. The journal recounts the experiences of the pair as they were held captive and subsequently released to resume their journey to Dublin.

Cork in 1750 was a thriving market town with links by sea to all parts of the European mainland. In describing the beginnings of the company, Frederick Nicholson, grandfather of the author, paints a vivid picture of a thriving community within a city very different from the one of the present day:

Opposite page: Bottles of red Burgundy, probably Beaune, being laid down to age in bottle before packaging as demand required, in the 1960s. Terry Connolly, seen here working in the cellars, was appointed Director of Purchasing and Operations in 1980.

The Royal Crest, awarded to those who have been appointed to provide goods and services to the Crown, or in this case the Crown's representative, the Lord Lieutenant of Ireland. The motto reads Honi soit qui mal y pense. (Shame to him who thinks evil).

"...we would behold a vastly different Cork to the city of to-day, a town bounded by or near what was later Patrick's bridge in the east, and Nile street in the west, almost like a Dutch town all intersected by canals and quays with the river Lee flowing up Patrick's street; with vessels unloading and loading at the quays, and across Daunt's Square to Castle street with a Kings castle at one end and a Queen's at the other with portcullis or water gate, whence the city's coat of arms." *Frederick Nicholson c. 1950.*

1750 saw the beginning of a long period of economic development and growth in Ireland which continued right through to the end of the Napoleonic Wars in 1815. Trade with Europe increased with exports of butter, beef and grain from Cork; capital began to be invested in indigenous businesses. The population began to grow with the heightened prosperity as infant mortality rates declined sharply. By 1800 the population of Cork stood at 80,000 rising to over 140,000 immediately prior to the Great Famine in 1845.

The business continued to develop throughout the later part of the eighteenth century and the early decades of the nineteenth. In the early 1820s Peter Maziere junior was joined by a Mr Richard Sainthill who became a partner in the business. Richard Sainthill's family originally came from Topsham in Devon; his father, Captain Richard Sainthill, was a career officer in the Royal Navy who served against the French before retiring and settling in Cork in 1793, dying in 1829. He was buried in Rathcooney churchyard, Co Cork. His son Richard Sainthill was a very well known numismatist (coin and medal collector) of the period, publishing a number of works on the subject. He was also instrumental in aiding a number of authors of the day in publishing their work for a wider audience. He was a "freeman" of the (former) borough of Ardfert, Co. Kerry and was one of the last of the "Common Speakers" of Cork, an honorary municipal office, now extinct.

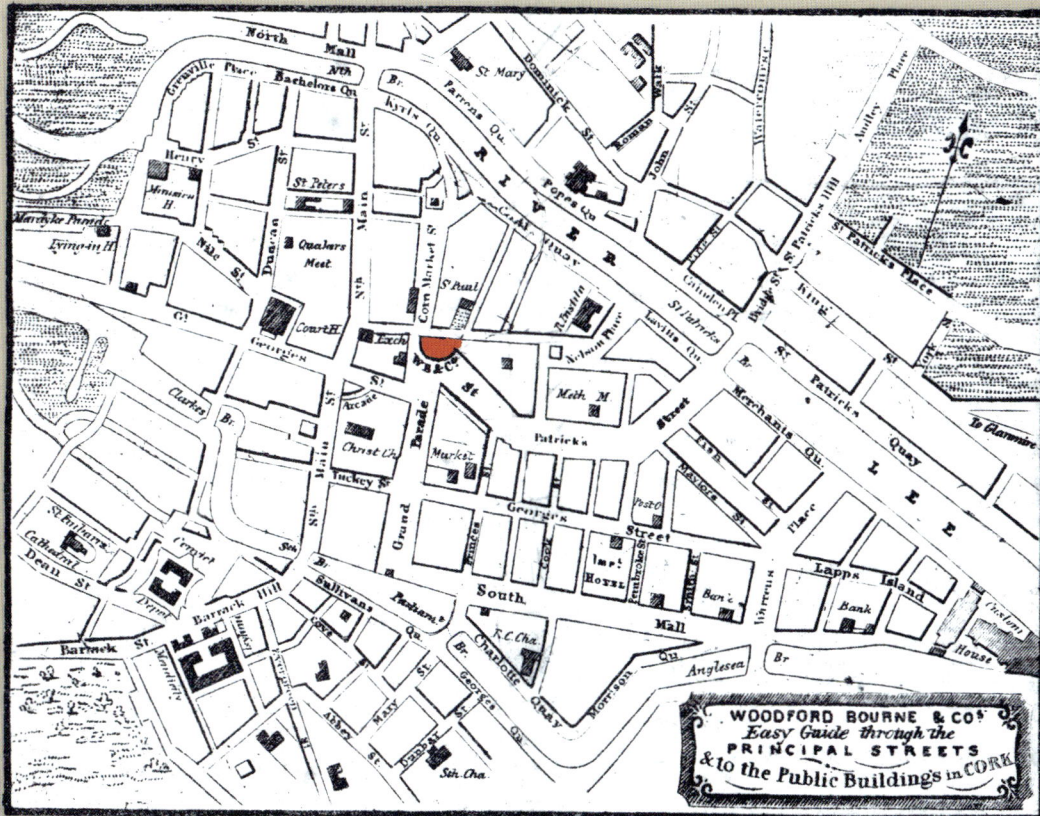

A map of Cork city taken from the company's Christmas catalogue dated 1849, clearly showing the central location of the Woodford Bourne premises.

In 1824 Peter Maziere died leaving the ownership of the business to his partner, Richard Sainthill who continued to develop it under his sole proprietorship. It was one of twenty businesses supplying wines, spirits and porter in Cork city. It was during this time that Richard Sainthill and James Adams Nicholson became acquainted. The principal product for sale was Irish whiskey distilled by a number of companies in Cork and Dublin at the time: Wyses' of the North Mall, built by Francis Wyse in 1779 and later merged into the Cork Distillers Company Limited, and the Glen Distillery at Kilnap which produced a fine malt, were two such establishments. Indeed brewing and distilling was one of the main industries in the country in the 18th and 19th centuries. Growth in these industries was mirrored by a recession in the woollen industry as production switched to Britain and the cotton industry in Lancashire began to grow in importance. With the development of the railway network in the 1830s and 1840s, raw material and the finished product could be readily transported throughout the country. Progress on land was matched by that at sea as ships were fitted with steam power, significantly reducing journey times and increasing trade and commerce.

A magnificent ten foot tall mirror, in perfect condition. This work was commissioned in the early 1900s after the formation of the limited company in 1904. The company was appointed with a second Royal Warrant in 1911.

The origin of the grocery side of the business was a firm called T Morley and Co. of Patrick Street which became Woodford and Co in 1838, directed by Mr John Woodford and based at 5&6 Grand Parade, Cork. The business was managed by a Mr James Bourne, selling a wide variety of teas, coffees, jams, imported sweets, sugar and biscuits. The principal product at the time was loose leaf tea which would have been imported, blended and packaged. Tea was sourced from Africa, India and China. Coffee was imported from Costa Rica and Peru. The additional variety and breadth of these product ranges were made possible by the developments in transport and the resulting reduction in costs.

The years 1845 to 1850 saw the Famine in Ireland with much suffering in Cork City and County, which was mirrored throughout the country. The resulting human tragedy initiated successive waves of emigration to North America; the population decreased from 8.2 million in 1841 to 6.6 million ten years later. Involved with philanthropic and charitable work in Cork City, Mr Woodford died in 1847 following a fever contracted due to his work with the famine stricken poor. Following an interval of some years, James Bourne married John Woodford's widow, taking control of the business which was renamed Woodford Bourne & Co in 1850.

The business continued to develop; in 1855 it secured a unique and prestigious award of a Royal Warrant to supply grocery products to the Naval Base at Haulbowline and the military barracks in Cork city. The appointment was as "grocers to his Excellency the Earl of Carlisle at Dublin Castle". This was following a similar appointment of Kinahan and Company Limited in Dublin, to supply her Majesty the Queen in

Photograph of staff and management alongside their new delivery van, one of the first of its kind in Cork, taken circa. 1915.

March 1845. As the business continued to grow, James Bourne appointed James Adams Nicholson to manage it. James Adams Nicholson was born in Maidenhead in England, the 8th son of the family. He was sent by the Royal Post Office on promotion to Cork as Post Master General in the 1850s. While in this appointment he came into contact with the owners and tradesmen of Cork city, among them the owners of Woodford Bourne.

In the late 1860s James Bourne retired to England leaving James Adams Nicholson in charge of the day-to-day affairs of the business in Cork where he received instructions by letter from James Bourne on the most important issues such as staff hiring, pay and commission. The company traded from 5 and 6 Grand Parade and 64/65 Patrick Street, selling a wide range of grocery items primarily to the professional and merchant classes in Cork and to the owners of the larger houses in the surrounding countryside.

In 1869 Richard Sainthill died leaving a considerable estate of £6,434 [2005 €630,000]. Upon his instruction, should the business not be taken on by his heir and namesake, his company of Maziere and Sainthill was to be sold to his friends Bourne and Nicholson who continued to use the premises at Falconer's Lane as a wine warehouse. In the event the business was purchased by Bourne and Nicholson and brought the grocery and wines and spirits concerns together, a commercial partnership that was to remain in place for over the next 100 years.

Front Cover Illustration:
watercolour of 5 & 6 Grand Parade
and 65 Patrick Street, Cork City,
by the artist R.B.Beattie
from Belfast.

This landmark building was designed
by Henry Hill (1806 – 1887) and
the construction was completed
around 1840. On a trip to Cork, it
caught the eye of R.B Beattie, an
accomplished artist from Belfast.
A perfectionist for detail, he created
a scene depicting the era of the early
1900s. He always liked to have
people in his paintings. The first
floor of the building accommodated
the offices of Woodford Bourne,
throughout its history. His widow,
Elizabeth, has kindly granted the
author and owner permission to
reproduce this work.

CHAPTER 2

The Foundation Stone

The First Generation

*D*ue to the expansion resulting from the purchase of the business of Maziere and Sainthill, and encouraged by the buoyant economic environment, Woodford Bourne and Co. built a new warehouse in Nile Street (now Sheares Street), in Cork city. This fine warehouse was commissioned in 1873 and completed two years later in 1875 at a cost of £4,500 [2005 €440,000]. The warehouse, which had a floor space of 28,000 square feet, was built from limestone with the thick floors and roof beams made from imported Canadian white Pine to support the great weight of the full casks. Special piling was constructed for the foundations, the site previously being a river. Inside, cut stone and arches surrounded the cellar area which was designed to hold casks and containers of varying sizes. Butts (110 gallons) of Sherry, Hogsheads (54 gallons) of Claret and Pipes (112 gallons) of Port and Marsala, were brought from the banks of the nearby river. An excerpt from Stratten in 1890 describes the warehouse:

"The wine stores and bonded stores of the firm represent a block of gable-roofed cut limestone, two-storey buildings fronting on Nile Street (now Sheares Street) and taking in the entire space from one of the smaller city arteries to another. The bonded department is a model of its kind…"[1] p153-154. *

The casks were kept under bond until their contents were required for bottling. Bottling was undertaken on the premises in specially controlled conditions replicating those in the cellars of their country of origin, with an even temperature and controlled humidity level. The cellars were divided into wet and dry with approximately one third of the total area being allocated as bonded space. This was controlled by the resident customs officer, who, along with the warehouse manager, had a key to the bond. Duty was assessed at the time of bottling and paid, releasing the product to the duty paid area of the cellars for bottling. The final products were then labelled before being sold through the company's retail premises in Grand Parade and Patrick Street.

✳ Information on footnotes throughout the book can be found on page 108

Opposite page:
John Woodford's widow, Jane, who was probably married to James Bourne when this canvas was painted by James Brennan R.H.A.

The Family of James Adams Nicholson, circa 1883. The author's grandfather, Frederick Norman is seated in the middle row with his hands clasped together.

Records of the imports of the company's wines since 1871 were meticulously kept in flowing longhand. Entries continued right up until the conversion of the Sheares Street warehouse in the 1970s, giving an accurate idea of market trends throughout this time. For example during the period from 1876 to 1878 the company shipped and bottled large quantity of wines from the continent, mainly Sherry, Port, Marsala and Claret.

At that time Sherry shipments came from Cadiz and were only pale and golden at a cost of 18/= to 24/= per dozen bottles for pale and 30/= and 35/= for golden. Later in the 1880's a wider range was imported including Amontillado, Brown, Manzanilla and also Montilla and the odd cask of Madeira. Luis Gomez of Puerto de Santa Maria was the regular supplier. Their sherries were of good quality and value and they continued to supply the company right up until the 1960s.

Large quantities of what was called "Bottling Port" were shipped from Oporto by Feuerheerd's at a cost of around 30/= per dozen bottles. This was an everyday drinking port as distinct from vintage port. Every few years, when the weather was suitable to produce a full bodied wine, a vintage would be declared. The company shipped vintage ports from the following years – 1896, 1900, 1904, 1908, 1912, 1920, 1927 and 1935. In 1899 records show the bottling of 10 pipes of the 1896 vintage under contract in London, presumably for sale ex the bonded warehouse in due course. In the late 19th and early 20th centuries shippers were mainly Taylors, Cockburns, Crofts, Warres, Kopke, Fonseca and Dows.

Marsala, a fortified wine like Madeira, is not readily available today, but in the 1870's it was one of the most appreciated fortified wines. Shipped from Sicily, it cost a mere 18/= a dozen. Marsala was shipped originally in Pipes but from 1890 onwards in Butts with the last shipment being recorded in 1932. This change in cask size might have followed a request from the British Isles whiskey trade who would have preferred butts for use in the refilling and maturing of whiskey.

In the 1870's claret (Red Bordeaux wine) was the drink of choice. The company received regular shipments in casks from Rosenheims and Eschenauer of varying quality at 12/= to 18/= per dozen bottles. 1895 saw the first imports of Burgundy and Rhine wines; Nierstein from Deinhards was the first white wine mentioned. By 1910 tastes were widening; Sauterne from Bordeaux and Emu wine from Burgundy which was bottled in flasks.

The Sheares Street warehouse which was completed in 1875, is one of the finest buildings in the city and is a listed building. Today it houses the modern Mardyke leisure complex and bars.

In total, the Woodford Bourne cellars would carry at any one time over 50,000 gallons of choice Cork and Dublin whiskeys, Scotch whiskies, fine French cognac, Jamaican rums and casks of wines, sherries and ports all carrying the marks of the principal continental growers. From 1887 the company had been registering the label designs of its wine and spirits brands both in England (for the export market) and at home. Labelling design was quite intricate, the company sourcing its label supplies from a UK printer. Trade marks were registered under such names as Iris whiskey, Brown Label for John Jameson and Sons whiskeys, Lion Crest, Lion Rum, Invalid Port and Invalid Brandy. This practice was encouraged by James Adams Nicholson who recognised the importance of product recognition and own or "house" brands where a quality could be guaranteed. In the development and protection of the products sold by Woodford Bourne and Co., James Adams Nicholson was ahead of his time.

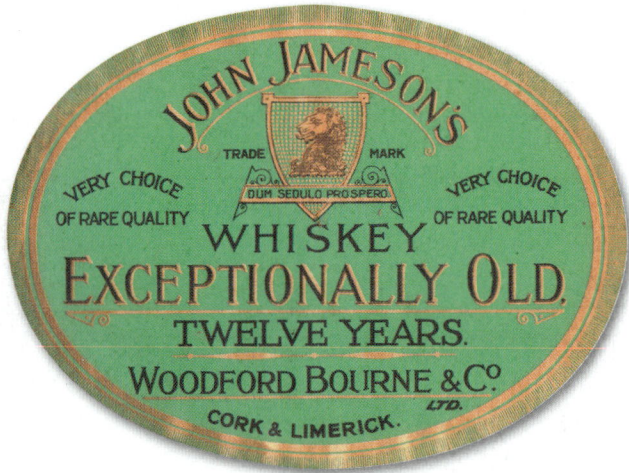

From the 1870s, the management of the company understood the importance of registering trademarks for labels and brand names. This is the "Lion Head in Crest" used for well matured Jameson whiskey.

Irish and English registered Trade Marks

1887	"Four Star Brandy" label for house brand cognac,
1900	"Iris" label used for blended Irish whiskey, mainly for export.
1907	Tea Pot design used on tea packaging,
1908	"Brown Label" label used for John Jameson's whiskey
1909	Lion Head in Crest (UK only) – embossed on many spirit labels
1910	Shield and Lion label – blank label for assorted Woodford Bourne spirit brands

Irish registered Trade Marks

1930	"Lion Crest" label – used for Scotch whisky
1945	"Lion Head in Crest" – embossed on many spirit labels
1963	"Toros Sherry" label – used for house brand sherry.
1964	Later Europa and Mirabeau, used for Cyprus Sherry and French table wines respectively.

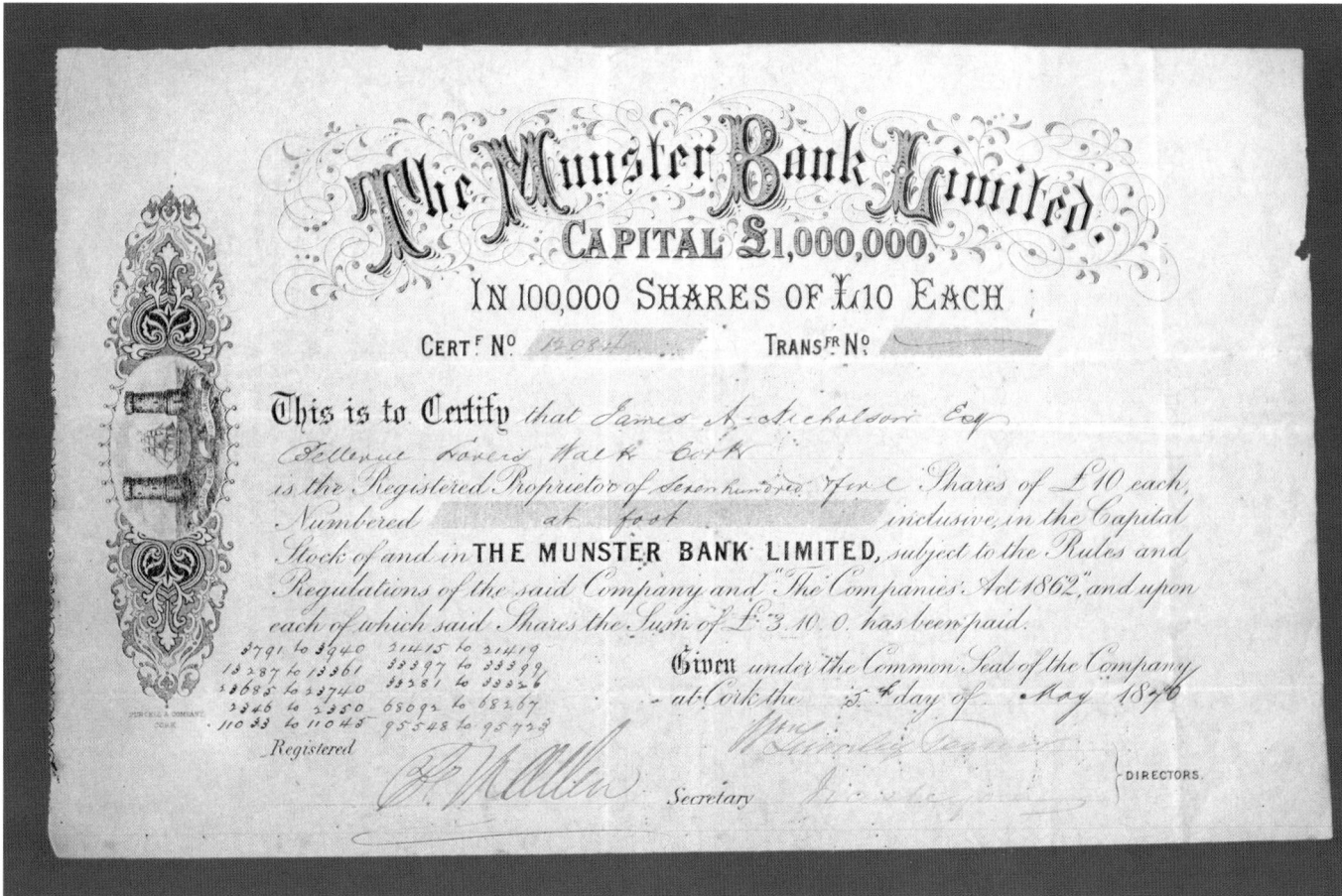

One of two Munster Bank share certificates which was owned by James Adams Nicholson.

This expansion of the storage and productive capacity of the firm matched the growth in the economy of the day as agricultural output rose steadily due to reorganisation and greater emphasis on beef and dairy production. The late 1870s however saw a world economic crisis with the collapse of agricultural production at home. Continued developments in transport and refrigeration meant increased competition from foreign agricultural exports. This period also saw considerable political unrest with the agitation for Home Rule, the emergence of the Land War in 1879 and emigration both to North America and Britain. However, difficulties in the agricultural sector of the time were mirrored by the development of the professions and local government in the towns, with the emergence of a merchant and administrative class who were the primary customers of Woodford Bourne.

During the 1880s the collapse of the Munster Bank was the first serious external event to threaten the continued operation of the company. James Adams Nicholson had subscribed, on behalf of Woodford Bourne, to two issues of Munster Bank stock in 1870 and again in

1880, to a value of £7,152 [2005 €740,000]. The Bank collapsed in 1885 leaving the bearers with no residual value on their original investment. James Adams Nicholson appears to have weathered this setback but it was to teach him a valuable lesson in investing in commercial concerns external to the company.

Not long after this incident, Bourne died in England enabling James Adams Nicholson to buy out the remainder of his shares from his widow. James Adams Nicholson was now the effective owner of the business, more than twenty years after first joining Woodford and Co as the shop manager. During this period he had overseen the expansion of the wine and grocery shop on Patrick Street and the daring investment in the new Sheare's Street warehouse which was to form the backbone of the company's operations in the years ahead.

Brown Label was the companies number one brand. Large stocks of young whiskey purchased each year would, when mature, be sold under the label. Initially Brown Label was a blended Dublin whiskey, but later it was marketed as a John Jameson whiskey product only.

During the remaining twelve years of the century, sales continued to grow in the city and county as demand increased from the British forces based in Cork. This contract was of the greatest importance to profitability during this period. Exports of whiskey to England were continuing to develop under the Iris label, the company appointing a London agent in 1895 to handle its overseas affairs and act as a sales office. Woodford's bought the young whiskey from a number of Dublin distilleries, transporting it to Cork for blending, bottling and storing in the warehouse at Sheares Street. This was a common practice at the time with the whiskey thus supplied maturing in the wholesaler's warehouse. Among the suppliers were George Roe and Company (founded in 1757), the Dublin Whiskey Distillery (founded in 1872) and W. Jameson Distillery (founded in 1752). Woodford Bourne's John Jameson brand was sold as "Brown Label – Dublin Whiskey", with their blended whiskey brand marketed under the "Iris" label. Rival merchants sold their Jameson under the following labels: Burke's "3 Star", Gilbey's "Red Crest", Mitchells "Green Spot". At the Cork Exhibition of 1883 McCarthy's of Cook St, Cork won a gold medal for their blended whiskey "Cloncarty" while most noteworthy in its worldwide distribution was Edward and John Burke's blended Irish whiskey.

Until 1890 Woodford Bourne sold its whiskey mainly in gallon jars to the retail trade locally. Later the Patrick Street shop sold all bottle sizes including a large amount of whiskey in small packs – ½ pints, naggins, babies which were bottled in Sheares Street. The Christmas price list was an unique presentation, prepared with much care and thought. Printed in good time, it was then mailed to the customers in Cork city, county and much further afield who would place orders for the festive season. In this way the company developed a thriving hamper trade. These were prepared and packaged in the lofts of the Patrick street grocery warehouse and Sheares Street wine and spirit warehouse prior to despatch. The company prided itself on its loyal customers and its "supply of widespread and influential clientele among the members of the titled nobility, gentry and clubs etc." [2]

In 1891, to reflect the growth in the retail trade, the company substantially remodelled its premises at 65 Patrick Street incorporating a new wine department. Reflecting its commitment to innovation, a gas engine was fitted at the Paul Street entrance to the grocery shop for electrical power generation in an emergency. The entry for the firm in Stratten's book (1892) describes with some detail the grocery and bonded warehouse operations, ending thus:

"All the affairs of the house are directed with marked ability, and its prosperity is fully assured by the honourable and thoroughly business like methods which to-day, as in the century and a quarter of the house's antecedents, characterise every phase of the administration." [3]

The interior of the company's Bonded warehouse, showing some whiskey casks and two Vats for blending spirits, taken circa 1940.

CHAPTER 3

The Challenge of the New Century

The Second Generation

By the beginnings of the new century, Woodford Bourne and Co. was a firmly established grocery, wine and spirit business on the commercial landscape in Cork City. The economic outlook further improved at the beginning of the 1900s with an increase in agricultural production which was to continue until after the First World War. Following the agitation and unrest of the late 1800s, Ireland experienced some political stability; the Land Act of 1903 encouraged many landowners to sell land to the tenants who farmed it. The conciliatory policies of the British governments of the time increased investment in transport and other infrastructure in Ireland, right up until the outbreak of war in 1914. Both the economic prosperity and political stability were good for business.

Trading out of the shop in the Grand Parade and Patrick Street and the Sheares Street warehouse, the company provided an ever increasing range of quality groceries and wines sourced in Ireland and England and alcohol from France, Spain and Portugal. Entries in the "Bottling Book" for 1901 show an increase in the sales of Claret and Port relative to twenty five years earlier, however sales of Sherry and Marsala had declined. In that year the company imported 1,100 Pipes (123,000 gallons) of Port and 2,200 Hogsheads (119,000 gallons) of Claret. Records for the period also show whiskey sales at 1,106 gallons for a six- month period representing 19% of total company unit sales.

Permission to bottle in Bond was finally granted from HM Customs in 1909. A dedicated bottling area was set aside and a glass lined vat with special blending equipment, filtering and bottling machines and a labelling machine were purchased. Bottling in Bond gave the company two advantages: firstly spirit spilt and lost did not include customs duty as would be the case if it had been bottled out of Bond and secondly, less capital would be tied up in stocks ready for sale as duty was paid once the items were "released". At the same time as the decision to bottle in bond was taken, spirit duties increased to 3/9d a gallon and continued to rise thereafter and became an increasing percentage of the cost of the goods. Board Minutes at the time show an increase in stable expenses over the period 1907 to 1909 following increases in the price of hay and straw!

Opposite page: James Adams, the first member of the Nicholson family to join the company in circa. 1860.

In keeping with its aim to expand the sale of quality food, a grocery store was set up in 1900 in O'Connell street, Limerick managed by Mr A.J Hayes who was paid 1/3 of the profits of the venture. This store sold similar quality products as the store in Cork, with its principal customers being the merchant and land-owning classes. The Directors of the company sent supplies to the shop from Cork and relied on the manager to run the day-to-day affairs. Trade continued over a number of years from the Limerick store, albeit on a limited turnover. Minutes from 1909 mention the trading difficulties of the store calling for the manager to be interviewed with the Directors expecting him "to bear any losses incurred in the future".[1] Board minutes record the continuing difficulties of the Limerick shop with special reports by the auditors highlighting continuing bad debts. However, from Board meeting records it would appear that Mr Hayes was committed to the success of the venture into the Limerick market, guiding the store through the difficult economic and political times. He was made a Director of the Company in June 1923, continuing in this capacity until 1936 when he resigned and was replaced by Mr John Talbot as manager of the Limerick shop.

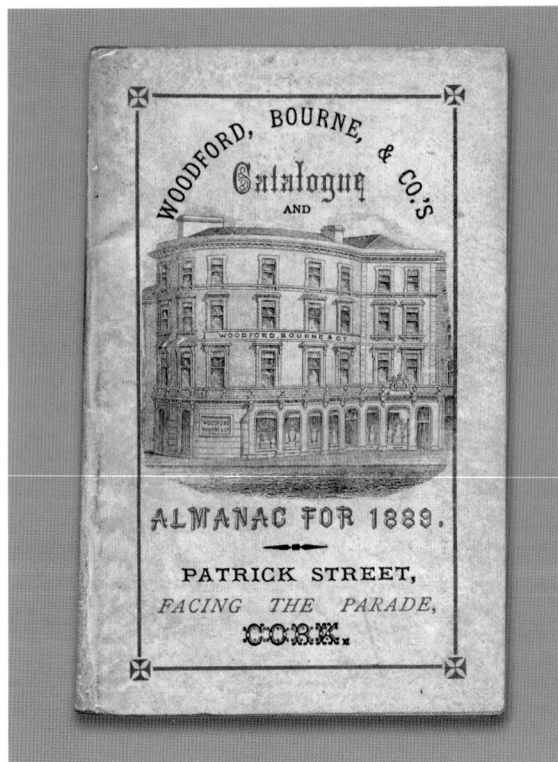

One of the Christmas Catalogues prepared each year since the 1880s. Customers were presented with a full list of products and prices.

In 1904 a new Limited Liability company was formed to take over the assets of the previous trading partnership of Woodford Bourne. The Articles of the Company list the objects for which the company is established as being "To acquire and take over as a going concern, and to carry on, either in Ireland or elsewhere, the trade or business of a Wholesale and Retail Grocer, Tea and Sugar Importer, Italian Warehouseman, Wine and Spirit Merchant, Dealer in Beer and Porter, and Manufacturer or a Dealer in Mineral Waters of all kinds...".[2] Board minutes for the period show the Directors of the company to be James Adams Nicholson (Managing), supported by three of his sons; Frederick Norman, Arthur Edward and Leo Septimus. A fourth son, James Warmington Nicholson, had previously worked in the business but died prematurely in 1903.

The share capital of the company was £60,000 with James Adams holding the Ordinary shares to a value of £30,000 complemented by an issue of Preference shares for the balance, held by the remainder of the Directors. The company entered into a financing arrangement with the Bank of Ireland who loaned £18,871 [2005 €2.0m] secured on the land and buildings of the business. Frederick Norman Nicholson was appointed Secretary of the Company. The first Board meeting of the Limited Company was held in July 1905. In the same year Atkins Chirnside based at 39 South Mall, Cork were appointed company auditors. The company was also further capitalised by a loan by the Bank of Ireland for £20,000, secured by a Debenture issue. Three years later, in 1908, James Adams Nicholson transferred his holding of 1,500 ordinary shares to his three sons Frederick Norman (600), Arthur Edward (500) and Leo Septimus (400).

Frederick Norman Nicholson, grandfather of the author.

This period saw the origins of another commercial problem that was to cause great concern to James Adams Nicholson and significant risk to the financial health of the company. In 1908, another two of James Adam's sons, Victor and Percy, set up the Britannia Motor Cab Company Limited with an issued share capital of £137,000. Based just outside London, this company manufactured taxi cabs for sale in the British market. This share issue was further supported by a loan from Lloyds Bank in London for £4,000 [2005 €470,000] which was guaranteed by James Adams Nicholson. In 1909 the minutes show a request for £500 [2005 €58,000] by James Adams from the Board, to cover the interest on the debt. By 1910, the problem had increased with James Adams Nicholson personally overdrawn as the demands of the bank increased. Lloyds bank sought the transfer of shares of James Adams Nicholson as security on the loan. This request was rejected by the Directors at a Board meeting in January 1910, but pressure from the bank continued.

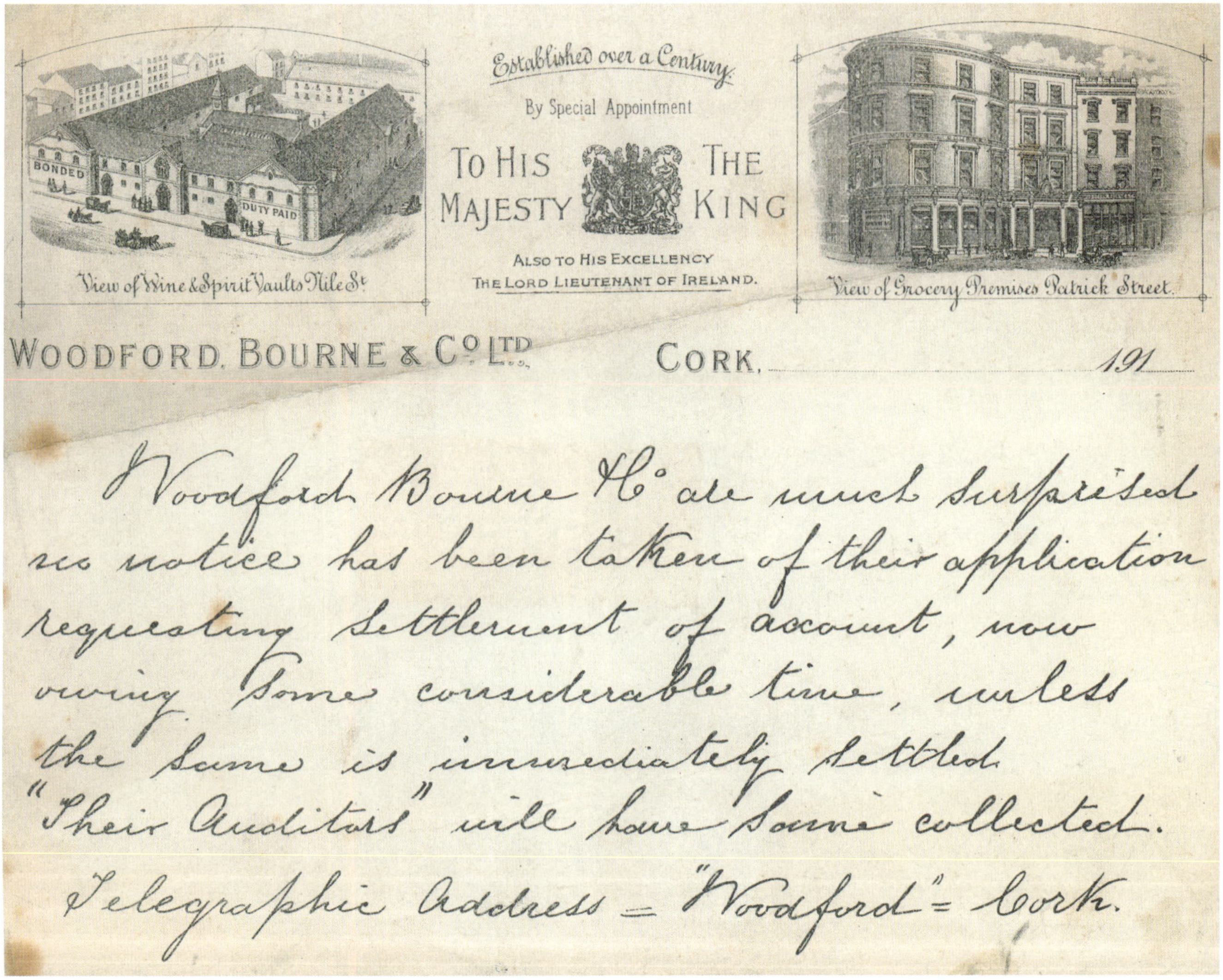

Established over a Century.

By Special Appointment

TO HIS THE
MAJESTY KING

ALSO TO HIS EXCELLENCY
THE LORD LIEUTENANT OF IRELAND.

View of Wine & Spirit Vaults Nile St.

View of Grocery Premises Patrick Street.

WOODFORD. BOURNE & Co LTD CORK. 191

Woodford Bourne & Co are much surprised no notice has been taken of their application requesting settlement of account, now owing some considerable time, unless the same is immediately settled "Their Auditors" will have same collected.

Telegraphic Address = "Woodford" = Cork.

A demand for the payment of an outstanding account on company notepaper showing the Nile Street (later Sheares Street) premises, Patrick Street premises and the right, granted to the company, to display the Royal Warrants.

The unrest and uncertainty surrounding the Britannia Motor Cab Company was solved with the setting aside of £4,000 [2005 €215,000] in war stock in August 1918. The resulting sale of the war loan in May 1919 enabled Woodford Bourne to pay off the remaining debt with Lloyds bank and the business begun by the two sons in England, was wound up. This represented the end of a significant risk to the company and to James Adams Nicholson personally as he had underwritten the security on the loans. He endured much pressure from Lloyds bank which was especially concerned with the security of the loan given the political unrest and changes of the time.

Woodford Bourne's business continued to grow with the introduction of salesmen journeys on a regular short rota to Cork city and the areas of Cobh, Kinsale, Monkstown and Spike

Island. The addition of a motor vehicle in 1912, opened up new routes to Crosshaven, Doneraile and Mallow. One can imagine the excitement at the arrival of this brand new motor vehicle for delivery and the very obvious promotional value of the clear lettering of the name and products of the company on the side. It must have been among the very first of its kind in the city. Later in 1924 another Ford truck was purchased, this time with pneumatic (rubber) tyres.

Orders were taken and notified to the premises on the Grand Parade and the goods assembled for delivery to mostly private residences. With the steady growth in business came growth in profits; 1911 shows a net profit of £891 [2005 €100,000] which rose to £1,714 [2005 €187,000] in 1912 and £1,647 [2005 €175,000] by the following year. Unfortunately the increase in business brought an associated increase in debts which were unpaid; minutes for 1910 show a bad debt level of £188 [2005 €21,000]. This development of the business continued to occupy the Board with extensive discussions on the success of the various routes or "Rounds" and the pay of the respective salesmen on each route. In 1914, minutes outline a scheme submitted by Arthur E Nicholson for commission to be paid to travellers on their respective rounds[3]. The use of commission-based wages was a common form of incentive used by wholesalers of the period, encouraging the acquisition of new accounts and the efficient servicing of existing ones. Woodford Bourne also insured all employees who collected money for the company in recognition of the risk they were taking in so doing.

In managing the family throughout this period, James Adams Nicholson resisted the various attempts by the Directors of the company to raise their salaries, increases of which had to be approved by the shareholders. Board Minutes of the time show that he was particularly

The new smart delivery van takes to the open road.

conscious of the ongoing requirement of the business to retain its capital to finance expansion and growth and feared demands by the shareholders (and the Directors) on the resources of the business.

Woodford Bourne, along with several other Cork companies was a large importer of tea. Existing company records go back to 1890 showing purchases of chests of tea and bags of coffee. The management sold their blends only in the Cork and Limerick shops. Supplies were sought from eight different English

companies including Peek's, Holborn's, Appleton's and Winch's. Blending took place in the dedicated tea room in the Grand Parade premises. Records for 1909 and 1910 show purchases of bulk tea at 48,295 and 48,340 lbs respectively. Indian teas from Assam and Darjeeling and Oolong tea from China all went into the resulting blends which were sold under different Woodford Bourne house labels for varying quality and taste. Blue Mountain coffee from Costa Rica was the most popular coffee. It was roasted in the Patrick Street shop for freshness, with the pungent aroma providing an additional attraction for customers.

To emphasise the continuing success of the company it was again honoured with a Royal Warrant as it continued to sell in quantity to the British forces. In 1911 Lord Stewart appointed Woodford Bourne with a Royal Warrant from the Lord Lieutenant, the representative of the Crown in Ireland. The warrant was awarded to all four family Directors of the company giving them the right to use the Royal Arms until all four were deceased. Thereafter the Royal crest adorned the letterhead of the company, during their lifetimes.

With the uncertain political environment in Europe, the economic situation in Ireland began to worsen with the approach of the First World War. Indeed the inflationary years that followed 1914 were followed by years of political unrest with the resurgence of agitation in support of Home Rule for Ireland. Changes in the political arena were also reflected in the government policies of the day, one of which was the introduction of taxation for private companies. Companies in Ireland became liable for Excess Profits Duty in 1914. This was renamed the Corporation Profits Tax after the end of the war in 1918, continuing as policy with the founding of the Free State in 1921.

Political events involved members of the family; Board minutes record the mentioning of Frederick Nicholson in the newspapers in connection with the Home Rule movement in a private capacity.[4] The further involvement of the family in the political events of the day was illustrated by the request to the Board for Arthur E. Nicholson to serve in the armed forces if called upon to do so. Initially this request was resisted by the Board, stressing the importance of his duties within the firm. The request was repeated at the outset of 1916 as the war in Europe intensified. Eventually Arthur Nicholson served with the British Army in Mesopotamia (now Iraq) returning at the end of the war to resume his duties with the company.

Records from the era indicate that Woodford Bourne was slow to increase prices in the inflationary environment, fearing an adverse reaction from its customers. Whiskey prices rose in 1916, coinciding with an application by staff for a general wage increase to compensate for a rise in the cost of living.[5] Demand for luxury goods such as wines suffered during the war years. In 1917 the company had to offload stocks at wholesale prices to the trade due to overstocking. Grocery margins also remained unsatisfactory during the period, with increases in the cost of imports. 1916 saw the introduction of whiskey rationing with a limit of one gallon per customer at any time. The company reluctantly raised whiskey prices in October 1917, with prices for a gallon rising 13%, from 36/= to 41/= . Price increases continued thereafter for the duration of the war.

The warehouse at Sheares Street always carried over ten years supply of Brown Label whiskey. The holding of such substantial stocks enabled Woodford Bourne to take advantage of the increased demand at home and, through the export of Iris and Brown Label, to meet the increasing demand of the British market. Annually the company would assemble the relevant number of Butts and Hogsheads to cover the quantity in gallons of the new young whiskey

Woodhouse was one of the leading exporters of Marsala in this era. Sadly to-day this fine fortified wine from Sicily is seldom available.

The Story of Woodford Bourne

Christmas Catalogue for 1916.

fillings to be provided by John Jameson. Both freshly emptied sherry casks and plains (those which had stored whiskey before) would be coopered (repaired) where necessary before dispatch to Dublin. The filled casks on return to Cork would be stored in the company cellars for seven to ten years and more to mature. Increasing sales of whiskey at higher process resulted in much improved profitability. Records show profits in 1917 of £1,580 [2005 €98,000] rising to £9,184 [2005 €400,000] in 1920.

As an insurance against political unrest, in May 1918 the directors of the company sent 50 Butts of whiskey to be stored in Bond by W.P. Lowrie and Co. Ltd, Glasgow, Scotland.[6] This act indicated the prudent nature of the management of the company which faced a post-war recession in Ireland and in their only export market in England. The post-war environment also brought worker unrest with union demands for a wage rise in 1919 which was granted but at the cost of the annual Christmas bonus! Records of the time also show the convening of a special meeting to consider the attendance (or lack of) of Leo Nicholson, one of the Directors. Following some deliberation it was agreed to pay Leo a salary directly linked to the time he spent working at the firm. Maybe less time spent on the snooker table in his favourite club was the order of the day for him!

After the First World War the first consignment of wines in bottles arrived from France; six cases of Chateau Lafite-Rothschild. Further varieties were imported to satisfy the demand, including Chablis from Burgundy, and Graves and St Emilion from Bordeaux. This represented a significant departure for the company which had heretofore imported almost all its requirements in cask and bottled the wine in its cellars in the Sheares Street warehouse. However the demand for Marsala wine decreased while that for fine wines developed as customers sought wines from well known vineyards in established French regions.

Working to the last, having seen many changes in the company, James Adams Nicholson died in July 1920 at the age of 88. The father of 11 children, three of whom were involved with the business at the time of his death, this entrepreneur and pioneer had developed and consolidated the Woodford Bourne company. From his initial employment with Bourne and through knowing Richard Sainthill he had developed Woodford Bourne into a thriving retail grocery and wholesale wine and spirit business. His building of the Nile Street (later Sheares Street) warehouse; his stewardship of the business through the First World War, the difficulties associated with the collapse of the Munster Bank, and the commercial failure of the Britannia Motor Cab company, demonstrated his vision, dedication and commitment over a period of fifty years.

Hydrometer set used by the Customs Officer in a Bonded Warehouse to measure the strength of spirits and thus establish the Excise Duty payable.

CHAPTER 4

Cautious Optimism

The Third Generation

Upon the death of James Adams Nicholson in 1920, Frederick Norman Nicholson succeeded him as Managing Director of the company, supported by his brothers, Arthur Edward and Leo Septimus. Frederick was a kind man, full of fun who was dedicated to the continued progress of the company. He lived in Glanmire, Co Cork in a house which has since become the site of the well known Flemings Restaurant. As he was taking over political and social events of the time were radically altering the trading environment for the company. The end of the First World War and the subsequent success of Sinn Fein at the polls in 1918, had culminated in the War of Independence and the foundation of the Free State in 1921. These years were ones of considerable uncertainty for traders and business owners of the day; only after the end of the Civil War in 1923 did normality return. The Civil War was fought with considerable ferocity, especially in Cork city and County.

With the passing of one generation, preparations were being made for the introduction of a new one. The issue of family working in the business was discussed at a meeting of the Board in December 1923 and a policy agreed among the Directors. The primary condition was that "…no son could take a position in the firm, receive money from the firm or interest himself in the business of the company except under the conditions of entry as may be passed by resolution of the Board." [1]

The subsequent conditions of entry proposed were the following:

- The son cannot expect at any time during his fathers service to receive higher remuneration from the firm than the salary of a manager,

- He must do one years apprenticeship from the date of resolution,

- He must be willing to work in any department as advised by the Board,

- He must enter through a written application stating that he is willing to abide by the resolution.

Opposite page:
A colourful leaflet that offered trial orders of the blended whiskey brand "Iris". Reasonable success was achieved in the British as well as the home market.

During the next decade Frederick Norman Nicholson was joined by two of his three sons. In 1922, Victor Brodie Nicholson entered the business direct from school, starting in the grocery department. His elder brother, James Frederick Nicholson joined the business in 1929 as company Secretary. James Frederick had previously graduated from Trinity College Dublin with a B.A Degree in 1916, immediately volunteering for the British Army where he saw service in the Transport Division in Mesopotamia (now Iraq). Returning at the end of the war, he graduated with an M.A Degree from Trinity College Dublin in 1920, before entering a chicken business in Cork. Two years later he passed his exams to qualify as a member of the Chartered Institute of Secretaries. James, or "Jim" as he was known to his friends was a talented golfer who won the inaugural Cork Scratch Cup in Cork Golf Club in 1923. He was also captain of the team from Monkstown golf club which won the Barton Shield in 1933. Frederick Norman's youngest son Dermot, also a graduate of Trinity College Dublin, was tragically killed in 1929, at the age of 23, on his motor cycle when he hit a fallen tree on the open road. He was an experienced competitor and a prominent member of the Cork Motor Cycle Club.

The years immediately following the death of James Adams were difficult ones for Woodford Bourne due to the civil and political unrest at home and continued recession in Britain. With the signing of the Act of Independence the company lost the lucrative government contracts to supply the barracks in Cork. The records also show continuing trading difficulties for both the food and wine departments; overall net profit of £6,200 [2005 €360,000] for 1923 declined drastically to a net loss of £180 [2005 €10,500] for the following year. Indeed, the civil unrest often took on a direct form for the company. Records for March 1923 show the holding up of the companies' one ton Ford van by armed men in Nohoval, Co. Cork. Troops from Kinsale were duly despatched and were successful·in sorting out the problem.

The warehouse at Sheares Street, built in the 1870's was the hub of the companies bottling, storage and distribution operations. The building covered a footprint of 28,000 square feet, with a yard and stabling at the rear. The entire site was bordered to the south by Washington Street, the east by Ann Street and west by Little Hanover Street.

10 years' stock of whiskey would be held in the Bonded areas. The company also held stocks of Scotch whisky (Lion Crest), Cognac (4 Star Label) and Jamaica Rum (Lion Label). Locally Brown Label whiskey was by far the largest selling product and special care was taken by the cellar master, Archie Keating, to see that each year's purchases were stored partly in the dry

The author's father, James Frederick Nicholson, a man of great understanding and patience. These qualities stood him in good stead when tackling unhappy and sometimes difficult shareholders.

and the wet cellars. The damp conditions provided a soft mellow whiskey with ageing, ideal for blending. When seven years old, the whiskey became mature for bottling; the directors then would pick a range of casks from which samples would be drawn.

After "nosing" those chosen would be blended together in a large vat and pumped back into casks to "marry" for six months. Further tasting followed, before this blended whiskey was pumped into the bottling vat where it was reduced to the permitted selling strength and coloured with special caramel to the exact shade. Bottled and labelled and packed in wooden boxes, the casks then had to be sealed for customs. This process guaranteed continuity of quality which established a following for Brown Label with those really appreciating fine whiskey. Annual losses of spirit due to natural evaporation of up to 2%, were allowed to the merchant. Anything over this level and the company was liable to the customs for the duty involved unless it could prove it was not consumed! Similarly a loss on the bottling operation was allowed at 2% without penalty.

Stoneware jars used in the 1800's for the sale of spirits.

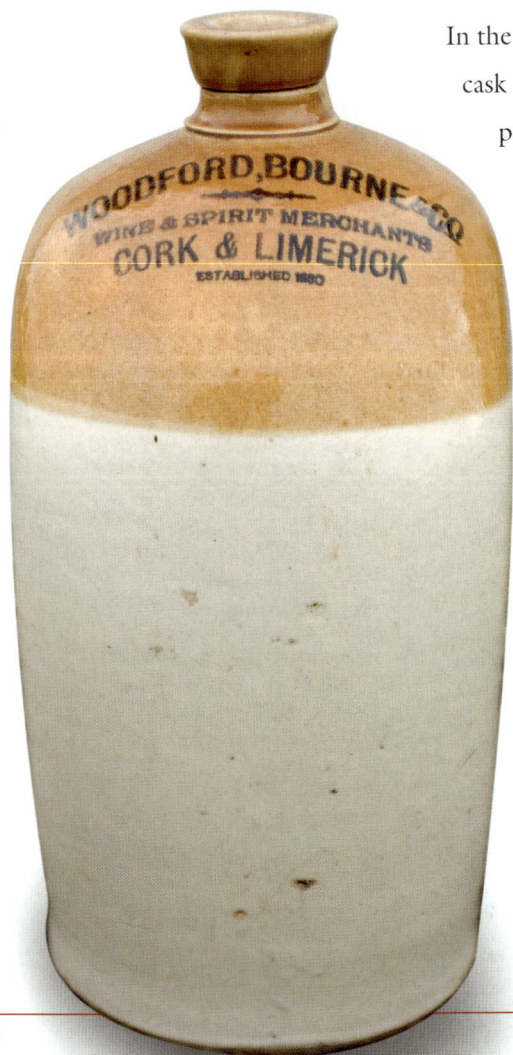

In the case of Sherry (Toros label) and Port (Country Club label) the entire cask would be duty paid in cask and set to rest on a stillon (rack) for a period to settle before bottling. These products, due to their fortification with brandy, could be left on ullage and quantities bottled off as needed. The casks would be fined and cleared with egg white, then bottled and labelled as required. Vintage port was bottled and laid in the cellars to mature further.

Table wines were duty paid and bottled with filtration as soon as possible. The corked bottles would be stored away in the cellars to improve in the bottle, some over several years before being offered for sale. Clarets and burgundies would be aged for some time with many having been pre-sold (en primeur) to customers. German wines were shipped in steel barrels and were very difficult to bottle. These would need to be stabilised with the correct amounts of sulphur to prevent fermentation. Terry Connolly, who worked in the warehouse at this time, remembers the atmosphere of the day:

"When bottling rum the bond would be filled with the aroma. There was usually a bottling in mid-summer of 5 gallon jars in preparation for Cork bakers and confectioners F.H. Thompson and Sons Christmas export orders, with the distinctive smells filling the warehouse. The place would be a hive of activity; noises from the bottling machines, people hammering on corks, timber casks being filled and stored and individually stacked on account of the absence of pallets in those days."

Stout, beer and lager were bottled and labelled in the duty paid area on an on-going basis with very large stout bottling in late autumn in preparation for the Christmas trade. Stout would be left for between three and six weeks after bottling otherwise it would pour flat. Sizes would be ⅓ pint (Invalid stout) and ½ pint. Grahams Golden lager was also bottled, being one of the few lagers on the Irish market at the time. After bottling it would be stored in cold water for a number of days.

Stout and lager arrived in barrels which were stored in the barrel yard. Empty barrels were sold mainly to farmers who purchased them at prices between £2 and £5. Some casks and steel barrels were returned to Spain and Germany. Terry remembers the practice of "recycling" (an unknown word then) which was important to maintain the supply of bottles for the bottling line:

"In the 1950s and 1960s bottles and casks were reused over and over again – customers received a refund of 2 pence for each bottle returned. We also had two men who went around town with box cars collecting bottles which Woodford's would buy at the bottle yard. Their names were Bottle Dan and the Blackman.".

Machinery was usually British in origin with expert hands required to keep it running. Bottle washers, fillers, corkers and labellers were all required for the full operation. Quality control was achieved by examining every bottle through light at the labelling bench. Wines from the cellars would be tasted prior to release by David Nicholson, Archie Keating and Sean Murphy.

Production volumes were made up each day by referral to the orders on hand and the stock on the premises. All bottling was noted in the bottling book with the bonded warehouse controlled by the "bond book". All goods were released from the bond on the drawing up of a customs warrant. Stocks and duty payments were controlled by large stock books which were entered up by the regular officer and checked by another later. This applied to all goods coming in, bottlings and withdrawals.

Stock was stored either in casks or in cases (of wine) again with the amounts being recorded in the bond or bottling books for those held under bond or stock held in the duty paid area.

JOHN JAMESON & SONS
EIGHT YEAR OLD,
PRICE, 20s 6d PER GALLON.
WOODFORD, BOURNE & CO, call special attention to their Eight Year Old Dublin Whiskey as being something very choice, and for which there is increasing demand.
WOODFORD, BOURNE, & COMPANY.
CORK. 133

BIRTHS, MARRIAGES, & DEATHS

The Cork Examiner.

NO. 13,119 Registered for transmission both in the United Kingdom and abroad.   MONDAY MORNING, JANUARY 14, 1895.   ONE PENNY

LADIES' AND CHILDREN'S UNDERCLOTHING.
LADIES' ALPINE WOOL COMBINATIONS 4s 6d, 5s 6d, 6s 6d, 8s 6d, 9s 6d, 10s 6d, 12s 6d
LADIES' ALPINE VESTS—4s 6d, 5s 6d,

LIEBIG
"COMPANY'S"
EXTRACT OF BEEF.
Makes the Best Beef Tea.

GREAT FALL IN PRICES.
FINEST LUMP SUGAR 2s per STONE
OUR 2/- PURE INDIAN TEA.

NOTICE TO THE PUBLIC.
DRIMOLEAGUE NEW FAIRS—Cattle and Pigs same day—will be held on the 18th of each month as follows:—January, February, March, April, June, July, and November.

WOODFORD,
BOURNE & CO.'S
DELICIOUS TEAS.
1s. 10d., 2s. 0d., 2s. 4d., 2s. 6d
133

QUEEN'S OLD CASTLE.

The company advertised in all issues of 'The Cork Examiner' & 'The Evening Echo' for over 100 years

The stocks of beers and duty paid spirits were checked by physical stock checks at the end of every week and the amounts referred back to the records to balance.

Orders were assembled in the despatch area against orders received and the requirement of the retail shop in Patrick Street. Stock for wholesale customers was usually sent by rail outside Cork with retail customers receiving their wine and grocery orders by county "rounds" to Cork city and county. Deliveries to the city and Monkstown area were made by horse transport; horses were stabled and groomed immediately behind the warehouse. This practice continued right up until the late 1950's.

The warehouse was staffed by a variety of people with specific tasks to ensure the smooth running of the day to day operation. However all jobs were interchangeable which was important to ensure continuity. The bottling line was manned by four people supported by young apprentices, with quality checking done by Archie Keating or Sean Murphy. Archie Keating also oversaw the bond supported by one other person. The despatch and stores area

Bottling in bond in the Sheares Street warehouse was an advantage to the company. The photograph, taken in the early 1930s, shows how it was done then and for some time thereafter.

was run by Seamus McDermott (to 1963) and Terry Connolly thereafter. The yard, stabling and horse deliveries were organized by either George Peilow or Tim Jeffers. Finally the van was driven by Danny O'Leary with maintenance carried out by Billy Deane.

The mid and late 1920s were prosperous times for the business with the recording of steady profit levels as economic growth picked up following the post-war recession. Board Minutes show a profit of £2,163 [2005 €124,000] in 1925, £2,573 [2005 €160,000] in 1927 and £2,428 [2005 €150,000] in 1929[2], despite the price deflation of the time. The continuing success of the company prompted the Directors to consider the purchase of the Glen Distillery based in Cork. This was to be financed by a loan of £9,000 [2005 €515,000] from the Bank of Ireland. However discussions in 1925 stalled because of the restrictions placed upon Woodford Bourne by the Memorandum and Articles of Association, so the idea was not pursued any further.[3]

The company advertised regularly in the Cork Examiner (now the Irish Examiner) taking the two ear spaces on either side of the title to publicise its grocery and beverage products. This contract for all issues of the Cork Examiner and Evening Echo had been ongoing since the establishment of the newspaper in 1840. Further efforts to widen its business in the Dublin market included promotion of a Dublin whiskey under the "Iris" brand. However the trading situation was made difficult with the introduction of tariffs in the early 1930s, making it almost impossible for the company to import many products which it would have otherwise. Relationships were fostered by sales staff who covered distinct areas of Cork and Limerick working on an incentive system based on sales and profits. The personality and persistence of the sales people was especially important as relationships when built, were long-lasting.

The succession of the business to the third generation was ensured with a number of new appointments to the Board. In 1929, James Frederick Nicholson and Victor Brodie Nicholson were appointed. In 1930, upon the death of Arthur Edward Nicholson, they were joined by Arthur's daughter, Irene Margaret (Peggy Ronan).

BY APPOINTMENT.

WHAT

Whiskey is Giving Satisfaction !

Woodford's
BROWN LABEL
Whiskey.

THE CREAM OF IRISH WHISKEY

EXTRA QUALITY

FULLY MATURED

UNIFORM QUALITY

Per Gallon, **25/6**
Per Doz. Bots., **51/-**

The famous Brown Label whiskey. A smooth whiskey, the very special care it received was rewarded by a loyal following.

In 1929 Peggy's brother Commander Vernon E.B. Nicholson O.B.E. joined the company for a short period of time having served in the Royal Navy during the first war. He rejoined the Royal Navy during the Second World War returning to Ireland in 1946. In 1948 he set sail for the West Indies with his wife and two children. Having safely arrived in "English Harbour", Antigua, he established "Nicholson Yacht Charter" in Nelson's dockyard, being the first company to offer this service. The business flourished with trade mainly from the United States. A radio station, chandlery and other associated trades were soon added. A friend to all mariners, his lively disposition was missed by all on his death in 1983.

The economic and political uncertainty of the day prompted some shareholders to seek reductions in the salaries of the Directors in 1932 and again in 1933. The calamity of the Great Depression, which had begun in 1929, was further exacerbated by the economic policies of the new De Valera Government initiated in 1932. The cessation of annuity payments to Britain triggered an economic war which lasted for much of the 1930s, with tariffs on cement and coal imported from Britain countered by those on livestock and dairy products exported from Ireland. Alleviation was achieved with the signing of the Anglo Irish Trade Agreement in 1937. Exports, which by 1929 had reached 35% of Gross National Product, were not to reach this level again until 1960, a generation later.

This period saw the third threat to the Woodford Bourne business (following those of the Munster Bank and Britannia Motor Cab Company) as disputes over shareholding and shareholders rights that had developed in the 1920's, manifest themselves in the early part of the 1930s. The business experienced a decline in profitability in 1930 to £502 [2005 €32,000] following a poor performance in both the grocery and wine businesses. The situation recovered slightly during the ensuing years prompting the managing director to put forward a positive note at the Annual General Meeting in 1932: "We can congratulate ourselves that our years trading turned out as satisfactorily as could be expected having regard to the prevailing depression." [4]

"THE EXTRA QUALITY'
JOHN JAMESON & SONS'
Very Old Whiskey,
Price, 22s. 0d. per Gallon.

WOODFORD, BOURNE & CO. have been fortunate enough to conclude a purchase with John Jameson & Sons for a very choice lot of their "Extra Old" Whiskey which has been lying in their Bonded Stores, Dublin, for a great many years, which is quite a *specialite*.
Those who really know and appreciate the brew of these celebrated Distillers will at once perceive the quality of the Whiskey now offered cannot be surpassed, if equalled. It is, as John Jameson & Sons' make, simply perfection. Woodford, Bourne & Co. are selling it at a very moderate profit, **pure** as received from the Bonded Warehouse, and warrant it the very finest quality procurable.
Sold in Casks, Jars, and Bottles of all sizes, specially labelled "Extra Quality." When ordering please mention "Extra Quality" required.
Price, 22s. 0d. per Gallon.

WOODFORD, BOURNE & CO.,
PATRICK STREET, CORK.

Up to 1900, whiskey was mostly sold in gallon jars and retailed in the Patrick Street shop for the price of 22 shillings.

In response to the shareholder unrest, in 1933 the Directors proposed and obtained a cut in the dividends on the preference shares of the company, with indications that they might not be in a position to pay dividends on the ordinary shares due to the economic conditions of the time. These events prompted some shareholders to seek further representation on the Board in an attempt to influence dividends and policy on Directors' salaries. The motions were defeated and the company saw a number of resignations from the Board. The difficulties prompted the re-evaluation of the shareholders register; ordinary shares in the company had been passed by James Adams Nicholson to his three sons two of whom died within twelve months of each other in the period 1929 and 1930. James Frederick Nicholson was given the task of purchasing back such preference and ordinary shares as became available in order to consolidate the ownership of the company. This was a lengthy and slow process conducted over a period of many years of often frustrating negotiations. However, by the late 1930s, ownership of the ordinary shares was concentrated in the hands of the Directors: Frederick Norman Nicholson, James Frederick Nicholson and Victor Brodie Nicholson.

Women shopping wearing the traditional shawl of the day- hence the name "Shawlies".

DIRECT
IMPORTERS
OF
PORTS,
SHERRIES,
CLARETS,
CHAMPAGNES,
MOSELLES,
HOCKS,
BURGUNDIES,
MARSALA,
TENERIFFE,
&c. &c.

CHAPTER 5

Barrels to Bottles

"The Importance of Whiskey is all"

The decade of the 1930s saw continuing development of the company. In 1930 the company had secured the contract to supply Irish Whiskey to all the hospitals in the Free State. In 1934 the Grocery and Wine premises at 64/65 Patrick Street and No 5 Grand Parade were extensively remodelled at a cost of £407 [2005 €30,000]. At the same time tenants were sought for the flats overhead, one of which was rented by Tom Barry, former Commander of the IRA in the southern counties of Ireland, who served in the First World War as did James Frederick Nicholson. James Frederick Nicholson took control of the wine department as well as his Secretarial duties, and Victor Brodie Nicholson was given the responsibility for the Grocery Department. Staff records for the time show seventeen full time staff in the business.

Woodford Bourne continued to develop and refine its product range with a concentrated effort on the marketing of Brown Label whiskey, including cinema advertising in the new cinema in Cork. Board Minutes show the allocation of £75 for advertising for the first six months of the year in order to achieve awareness of its products. However, political events conspired to undermine the successful efforts the company had made in weathering the storm of the Depression. The withdrawal of the British Navy from the local ports in 1936 came as a serious setback to trade, with the impact clearly visible in the profitability of the company. Records for 1936 show a loss of £1,022 [2005 €70,000]. However, despite this a modest profit was achieved in the following year. The Navy had been a customer since the 1850's, principally of marsala, claret and port.

Immediately prior to the start of the Second World War, in May 1939, the Distillers Group who exported to Ireland the top six selling Scotch Whisky brands, decided to hand over the administration of the quota system of the White Horse brand in Munster to Woodford Bourne. This in some way compensated for the setback caused by the loss of the naval contract. Based upon the previous sales achievements of each designated wholesaler, their quotas were distributed monthly by Woodford Bourne and were the subject of frequent

Opposite page:
The company was very proud to be a direct wine importer and from all available reports probably was the largest outside Dublin in the 1800s. Note the mention of imports from Tenerife, an island not known especially for its wines to-day.

requests to secure extra supplies. With additional stocks of this well known Scotch Whisky, wholesalers could secure extra sales of sherry and port as well as use the opportunity to sign on new customers. This arrangement continued until the early 1960s when the agency was transferred to a Dublin company, Jas. McCullagh, in which Woodford Bourne had a minority interest.

By the 1940s the company was supplying a limited number of outlets with its bottled Guinness, Smithwicks Ale and Jacob's Lager. Later Graham's Lager and Double Diamond were added. Some of these products were available in the larger shops and in selected Hotels in Cork such as the Imperial Hotel on the South Mall, but the significant trade was through the two retail shops in Cork and Limerick. More modern equipment was installed for bottling Guinness, as uniquely the company had an arrangement with Arthur Guinness and Sons to print their own Red label and were proud to have this special identification. This new equipment, and the attention to quality in manufacturing, ensured the stout was always released for sale at its peak. This attention to quality ensured that the product had a dedicated following in the Munster area. However the bottling of beer and lager was not without its difficulties as it was subject to "fobbing" or frothing resulting in the loss of gallons of beer, a problem that was never successfully overcome by the company.

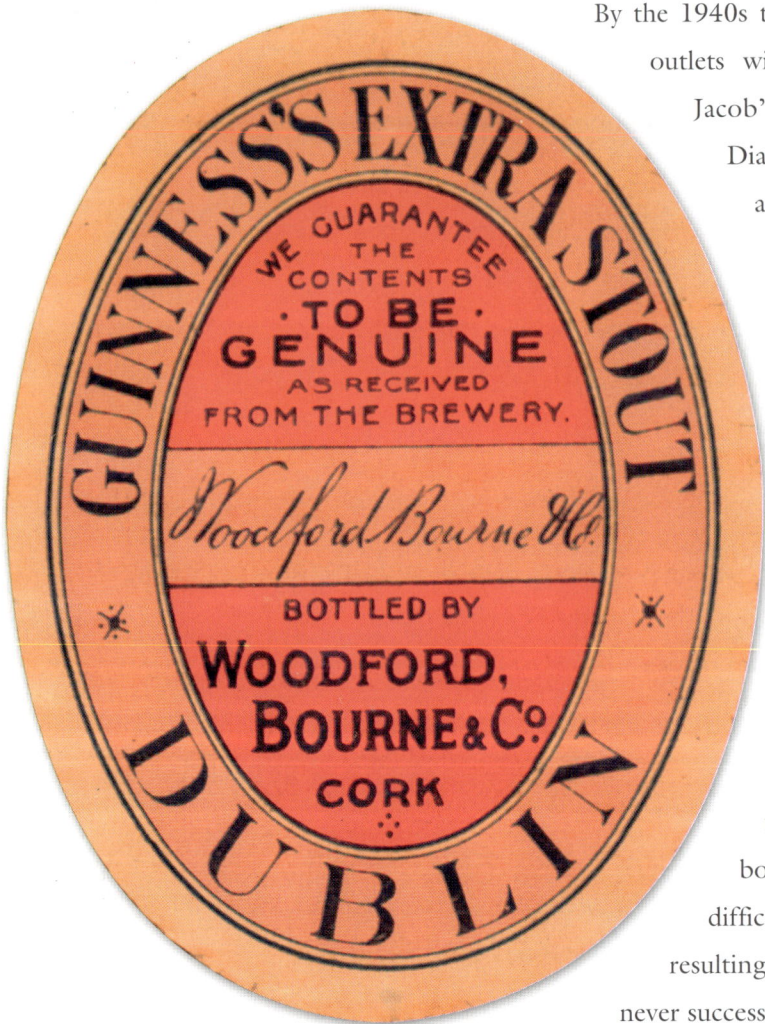

Red Label Guinness bottled and very specially treated by the company, was sought after by regular customers. Invalid size ⅓ Pint bottles were a prescribed tonic!

During the Emergency (as the war years 1939 to 1945 were known in Ireland) the company effected changes to the storage of its products in the Sheares Street warehouse; permission was sought and obtained from the Revenue Commissioners to extend the bonded (duty exempt) storage area. In a more bizarre development permission had to be sought to store buckets of water in the bonded areas so long as "…these casks were distinctly marked and officially sealed with the customs seal." [1]

The Patrick Street wine shop in the 1950s, with Michael Murphy serving in the background and Denis O'Driscoll about to wrap a quart bottle of Brown Label whiskey.

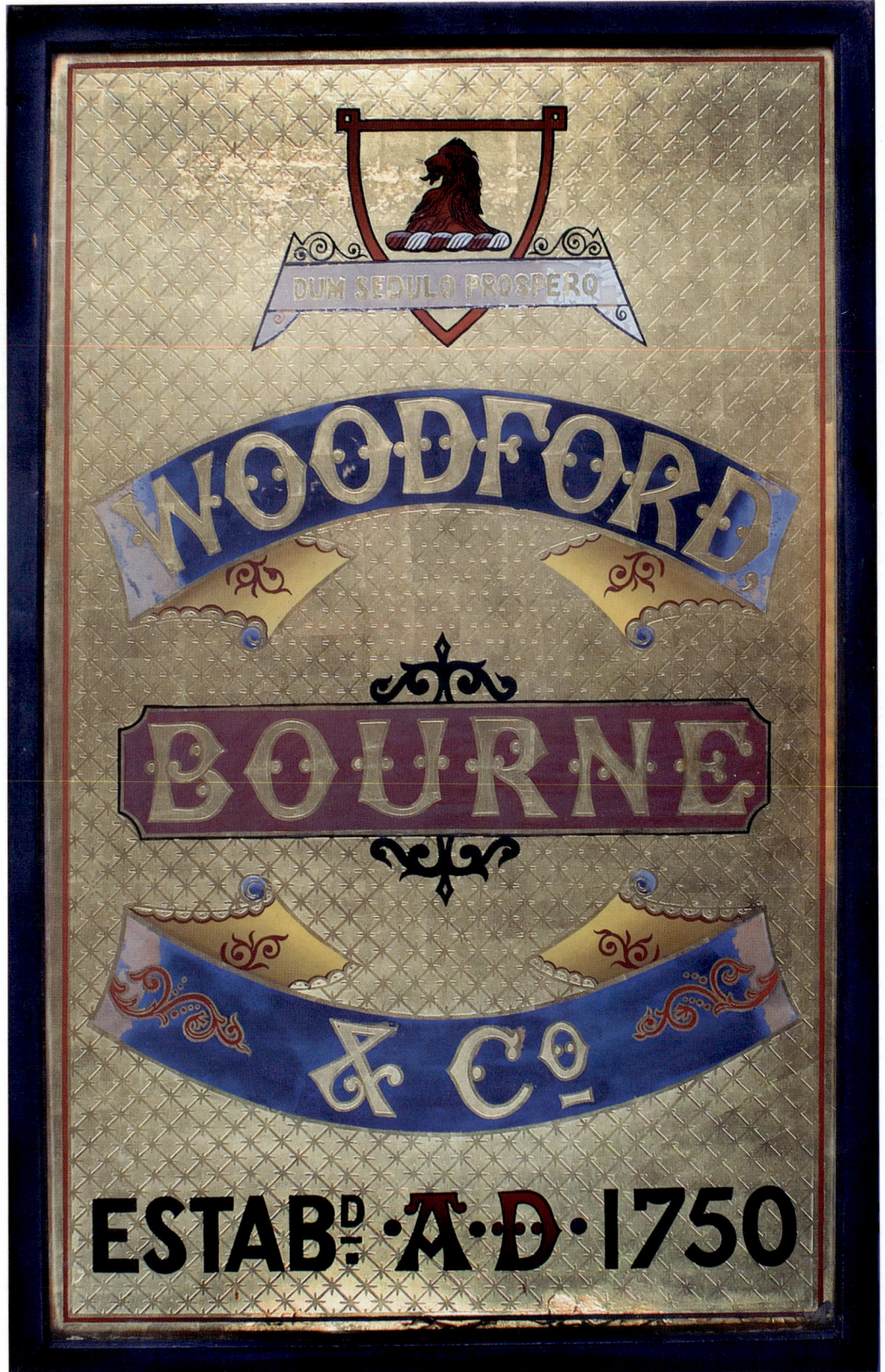

DUM SEDULO PROSPERO

WOODFORD

BOURNE

& CO

ESTAB^D · A · D · 1750

One of a pair of mirrors which adorned the walls of the Patrick Street premises in the early 1900s.

Meanwhile, the grocery business continued to grow slowly through the shops and from rounds of the salesmen in the Cork area. The range of products in the Patrick Street shop included blended tea and coffee (roasted in the shop window), dried fruit, sugar and cereals. The company also imported a large number of products including cakes and confectionary items from England. However sales of the business suffered due to the war and the rationing or unavailability of many imported goods, in particular tea, sugar and petrol. Rationing was introduced with the inevitable reliance on horse drawn carriage for the delivery of orders to the company's customers. During the remainder of the war the company continued to return profits, which increased in 1943 to a level of £2,496 [2005 €97,000] but declined to £1,463 [2005 €54,000] in 1945.

A close up of the label of the company's registered "Iris" brand which was showing some success in England prior to the 1950s.

The War halted wine imports altogether and it was not until late 1946 that an increasing number of chateau owners and exporters were beginning to supply in bottle. This development enabled importers, including Woodford Bourne, to expand their range and to sample wines from the then lesser known regions of France, including the Loire Valley and Alsace. Coincidentally, white wines were becoming more acceptable as customer tastes were changing and an increased interest was being shown in some of the dry varieties such as Chablis and Muscadet. The company responded to this development by including a much wider selection in the Patrick Street retail shop: from Piat and Lupe Cholet in the Burgundy region came whites – Chablis and Pouilly Fuisse, and reds too- Clos Vougeot, Vosne Romanee, Gevrey Chambertin and the less expensive Macon and Beaujolais. From Calvet and

A staff photograph taken in the late 1940s or early 1950s, outside the Queen's Old Castle in Cork city.

Included left to right front row are Bernard Murphy, Cissie Sparks, Eileen Daly and W.T.Smye.

Middle and back row - Archie Keating, Willie Warner, Seamus McDermott, Michael Murphy, Kate Murphy and Dick O'Reilly.

Eschenauer in Bordeaux came Chateau wines – Leoville Lascases, Pontet Canet and Beychevelle along with other wines from St Julien and Margaux. From the Rhone Valley came Cotes du Rhone, Hermitage and Chateau Neuf du Pape.

In 1953 Frederick Norman Nicholson, who was predeceased by his wife Sarah by several years, died at the age of 83, having attended to the business of the company right up to his death. He had ensured the continued success of Woodford Bourne throughout his tenure as Managing Director, covering the difficult years of the Great Depression and the Second World War. In 1950, on the bi-centenary of the company which happened to coincide with his 80th birthday, he was presented with the gift of a wireless set by the employees of the company with the following note:

"A wish was expressed among the entire staff that they should mark the occasion of the bi-centenary of the firm in some special manner, and it was thought that, your Staff could best show its pride in such an important event in the history of the firm, by extending to you our present managing director, a small token of our respect and esteem, and in appreciation of your many years as head of the firm. We are glad to remember that you Mr Nicholson are always ready to give a sympathetic hearing to any member of the staff who comes to you, and to give advice and counsel. We earnestly hope that you will be spared in health and strength for many years to come to continue as our managing director, and we ask you to accept this wireless set in the hope that it will give you many hours of pleasure, and also that it will remind you of an honourable achievement in the firms history."   Fred Norman Nicholson "Two Centuries of Progress" c. 1950.

Woodford Bourne succeeded in maintaining its profit levels in the years following the war and throughout the early 1950s. This was a period of increasing duty levels, economic difficulties at home and increasing emigration with 70,000 leaving the country annually. At the time of the death of Frederick Norman Nicholson, the era of the second generation of the family was drawing to a close. The business was still a profoundly traditional one centred on grocery retailing and delivery, wines, beers and spirits, with markets predominantly in the Munster region and with some customers in Dublin and overseas. The wine and spirits business, however, was experiencing a slowing due to the taxation policies of the government in response to the economic conditions.

By the mid 1950s a number of leading public houses and licensed shops in Cork City and Munster were stocking Brown Label whiskey and a scattering of other brands. Competition was tight as retailers were not inclined to change suppliers except where there was a customer franchise for a certain brand. For this reason "Brown Label", the company's labelling of Jameson whiskey, was particularly effective in developing and keeping trade. This period saw the start of the wholesaling business in the Munster region with a salesman calling to shops in the Munster area. The salesman took orders, discussed new products and provided the link between the shopkeeper and the wholesaler in the city. At the time there were numerous wine and spirit wholesalers trading in Cork city, including John Daly, M.D. Daly, D.F. O'Sullivan, J. McCarthy and Sons, Lee White and Co., Murphy O'Connor and Co. By the early 1980s all except Woodford Bourne and Lee White and Co had ceased trading (M.D. Daly having become a part of Grants of Ireland). Changing patterns of trade brought new entrants to the industry, with the revolution in Cash and Carry distribution and the large suppliers, in particular Irish Distillers, selling a full range of Irish spirits direct to virtually all shops and outlets of any size.

A pen drawing of the Oyster Tavern in Market Lane, Cork by Marshall Hutson. This adorned the front page of the Restaurant Menu for many years.

The success prompted the opening of a similar establishment in Limerick. The Brazenhead Bar and Grill opened in 1950 on the site of the former Woodford Bourne shop in O'Connell Street This had been closed in 1946 due to poor trading figures immediately following the War, with the premises being rented out in the meantime. The restaurant was run on the same style as the Oyster, with large crowds thronging the bar and restaurant especially after a day out at Limerick races. Management, from as far away as Cork, was always a problem and it never achieved the same dedicated clientele as its forerunner in Cork. None the less, many local business people and politicians were customers for over a decade.

CHAPTER 6

The Oyster Tavern

"Jimmy Martin, a legend in his own lifetime"

Within the context of the war-time difficulties discussed in the previous chapter, in 1943 the Directors made an important decision to enter the beverage and fine dining market in Cork with the purchase of the Oyster Tavern in Market Lane. From historical records the earliest trace of the Oyster Tavern dates back to 1792 with the uninterrupted development of the site as a coach house, pub and restaurant in the intervening 150 years. Historical records show that prior to 1828 a first class restaurant was run on the site, with ownership transferring a number of times subsequently. James Frederick Nicholson and Victor Brodie Nicholson recognised the opportunity to combine their knowledge of fine foodstuffs with fine wines to develop a quality restaurant business situated in the heart of Cork city. Once the legal papers had been signed, they set off together on a celebratory visit to the premises to be told, as they sat up on a bar stool, that the pub had just been sold, the staff not realising that they were talking to the new owners! A company was formed with the two brothers and John Elmes as Directors, with Victor Brodie Nicholson taking over control of the restaurant.

The restaurant soon established a top class reputation both in Munster and abroad, with a quality menu and wide range of fine wines, and became the venue of choice for lunchtime and evening dining in Cork city. A charcoal grill was incorporated in the mirrored dining room. Cuisine previously unavailable at that time in Cork was served, including char-grilled steaks, game and fresh seafood and Galway Bay Oysters. Initial staffing problems were overcome by the arrival of Jimmy Martin who took over the day-to-day control of the restaurant with enthusiasm and 100% commitment. Occasionally he was assisted by his daughter Margaret. "Mr Martin" as he was known to many, was without doubt a legend in his lifetime. Apart from a daily chat with Brodie Nicholson, Jimmy's word was law. He was strict but respected by the staff and insisted on organising all table seating arrangements himself. In particular, the Oyster was famous for its steaks, which were Jimmy's speciality. He hung and butchered the carcasses and then cooked them on the charcoal grill. He was known to call one of his assistants to summon a customer to be seated with the not to be forgotten expression "Call in the destroyed steak"! He always had a special word for the regular clientele, amongst whom was included the entrepreneur Ben Dunne. He maintained the highest standards right up until his retirement in the late 1970's.

Jimmy Martin, at the charcoal grill. From many years, from the 1950s onwards, a businessman's visit to Cork was not complete without a meal at this old tavern.

CHAPTER 7

Fine Wines Chosen with Care

The Fourth Generation

Conditions in the decade commencing in 1954 were instrumental in furthering the prospects of the company, particularly in the area of the embryonic development of the wine market thanks to the increasing availability and knowledge of fine wines and table wines for more frequent consumption. National economic conditions continued to be difficult during the middle years of the decade but there was an improvement with the publishing of T.P. Whitaker's seminal report on economic policy in 1958. With a new focus on free trade, increased exports and the attraction of foreign investment to Ireland, the new policy was to have profound national effects and benefited Woodford Bourne both with the new growth in the markets which it served and the expanded variety of products it sold.

In 1954 David Nicholson, the eldest son of James Frederick Nicholson, joined the business directly after completing a Bachelor of Commerce degree in Trinity College Dublin. Of the fourth generation to work in the business, it was natural that David would understand both the significant family heritage of the business and the challenges it faced. David wrote:

"In 1954 when I joined, the business was solid, with a good wine and spirit trade passing through our Patrick Street shop. The grocery struggled but overall after paying all staff and three members of the family there was little left at the end of the year for reinvestment. To my estimation working in the Sheares Street warehouse, the future looked uncertain. I realised how lucky I was to have a management job in such a long established business but as the young executive I would have to make things happen in the years ahead, if the company was to succeed long-term."

The preceding 25 years had seen economic stagnation, a lack of investment and innovation in industry and a declining market as many capable people emigrated. In the post T.P. Whitaker era the economy was opening up to new ideas and trends, and it became apparent that the most significant development for distribution companies would be the switch to self-service as customers sought the freedom to browse and purchase a wider range of products

The 1926 Eucharistic procession through Cork city, photographed as it passed the Woodford Bourne building, on its journey from the Monument, Grand Parade to the North Cathedral.

at increasingly competitive prices. A number of companies began to experiment with self-service in the mid 1950s, particularly in the Dublin market. Findlaters, H Williams and Dunnes Stores in Cork all began to attract customers in this way. The arrival of the fourth generation into the business coincided with the rapidly changing marketplace and the need for firms to innovate in order to survive. This was also at a time when non-family managers of considerable experience were retiring from the company. 1954 saw the resignation of W.T.Smye, a Director of the company since 1933, having been the second non-family member and company employee appointed to the Board. During his time as the manager of the Patrick Street store, sales had continually expanded. In 1954, James David Nicholson (the author) was also appointed to the Board, the fourth generation of the family to direct the company's growth.

Woodford Bourne continued to develop its well-established trade through the servicing of its customers by its grocery rounds in Cork city and county from its shop on Patrick Street. Items were packed and sent by van to Mallow, Buttevant, Ballincollig, Passage West, Monkstown, Cobh, Rushbrooke, Kinsale, Crosshaven and to all areas of Cork City. The Christmas trade, including exports to Britain, had been important for both the grocery and wine departments. However by the mid 1950s, this trade began to come under pressure from the smaller shops in the suburbs; figures for the grocery department show a decline in the delivery business as well as in the export business to Britain. This was caused by the trend to convenience and self service which was to define the grocery industry over the next 40 years.

Despite this, the range of products in the shop continued to grow from the base of tea, coffee and cereals. The company imported Huntley and Palmer's cakes and biscuits from Reading, Fullers' cakes, Sharwoods' conserves, Barker and Dobson sweets, McVities' biscuits. The shop also sold an extensive range of delicatessen products: ham on the bone, cheddar cheeses and French cheeses which were imported by air. David recalls: "Piano wire was used to dissect portions from the block of cheddar cheese. If this broke chaos ensued. The youngest staff member was despatched to secure a replacement to be sought from Piggot's music shop nearby while customers waited patiently for her return". The wine shop continued to seek custom through advertising in

A William the Fourth wine cooler with harepaw feet, dated 1835. Owned by the family, this is a fine piece of furniture with its sarcophagus shape and flat top.

8

8

James Frederick Nicholson (the author's father), seen presenting Cissie Sparks and Archie Keating with tokens of appreciation for their contribution to the company's progress over a long number of years.

the Cork Examiner and the carefully planned attractive Christmas list was awaited with interest each year. It contained details of mouth-watering grocery items and a specially recommended range of wines and spirits, all keenly priced.

The economic environment at the time was detrimental to rapid growth and the development of the company. However Woodford Bourne began to build upon its expertise in wine importing and distribution and in this the future seeds of its success were sown. Its first innovation of the period was directly into the tourist market to the returning Irish Americans. In the late 1950s the company began selling "5 Bottle" packs of whiskey, an American gallon, to these visitors who could import the packs under special license, duty-free into the USA. As agents for Jameson's, the company bottled and packaged the whiskey in bond at its Sheares Street warehouse. This was then transported under bond to the Cruise liners visiting Cork Harbour en route for America. Co-operating licensed travel agents throughout the country, especially on the western seaboard, would pass on orders to the company.

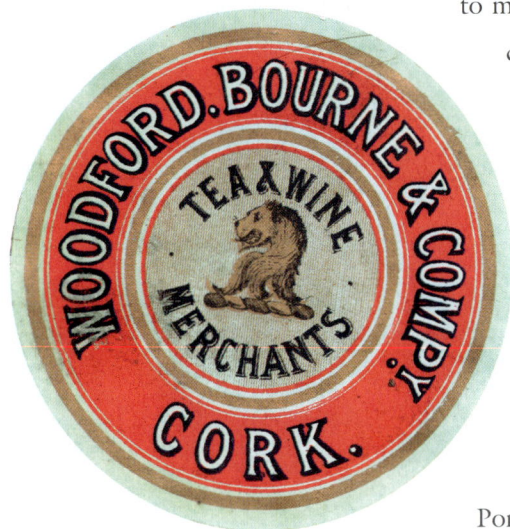

Woodford Bourne captured 80% of this trade, selling between 50 and 100 cases to most visiting liners. This continued for the next ten years while ships called at Cork. These business contacts in the west and south west of Ireland were to be helpful in developing the company's business in general drinks wholesaling some years later. The resulting extra sales revenue of some £11,000 [2005 €270,000] in 1957 along with the contribution from the White Horse agency was a substantial help to boost flagging profits.

The late 1950s saw the national development of the market for light unfortified wine – or Table Wine - with the establishment of brands such as Blue Nun from Germany and Mateus Rose from Portugal. This also coincided with the gradual switch to self service, giving everyone ease of choice from the increasing number of varieties on offer. Woodford Bourne had already built up a significant trade in Table Wines in its Patrick Street store, especially pre-Christmas, with long queues forming outside the shop. In 1959, in order to develop the product range and invest in the future, the company began purchasing young and immature fine wines for laying down for future consumption. From this time Woodford Bourne was establishing an extensive list of contacts in the French wine industry with regular visits by David Nicholson to the growers, exporters and co-ops in Burgundy, the Rhone, Bordeaux and the Loire vineyard areas. Occasionally visits would also be made to Rheims in the Champagne region and on to Alsace in the north for some fruity Gewurtztraminer.

The company was well respected for the quality of its range of teas. Brodie Nicholson had regular tasting of the various blends to maintain a consistency of flavour. It, along with coffee, was often advertised in the ear spaces of the then Cork Examiner. The labels depicted were affixed to the packets by the staff in the tea lofts.

In 1959, with advice from these wine experts, a limited range of fine wines were sold "en primeur" ie. in the first year of their life, before bottling and delivery some time later. The wines chosen were predominantly from Bordeaux, beginning with contacts in the St Emilion and Medoc area. The company started with some of the very finest 1st and 2nd growth clarets: Chateau Margaux, Chateau Lafitte, Chateau Mouton Rothschild and Chateau Cheval

Blanc (St Emilion). Wines from Burgundy were also purchased, including Nuits St George, Gevrey Chambertin and Pommard. This practice of the laying down of fine wines continued for much of the next fifteen years, with customers from the Cork locality and from the greater Dublin area. These wines were bottled mainly by the growers in their cellars in France, a trend that was to continue and develop as producers aimed to control the branding and quality at source. Exceptions to this were Chateau la Tour du Pin Figeac and Chateau la Fleur Figeac, both from St Emilion which continued to supply in cask direct to Woodford Bourne until the 1967 vintage. Many Port shippers including Taylor's, Cockburn's, Warre's and Fonseca, adopted the same strategy and offered their vintage port only in bottle. Woodford Bourne was also fortunate in having purchased and laid down large quantities of the recent vintages of 1955, 1960, 1963 and 1966 in their warehouse in Cork, which had been shipped in casks at a lower cost.

To support its expanding range of wines as well as Brown Label Whiskey, Woodford Bourne secured the Irish agency for Frapin Cognac from Segonzac in France. This was a very smooth cognac distilled from the grapes of the Grand Champagne area the region recognised for the finest brandy of all. The venture brought reasonable success but the product was in competition with Hennessy Cognac which already had a very established market position. An innovative promotion with a vintage car brought over to Ireland to gain press publicity helped but only modest gains in the market were achieved. In the mid 1950s Vermouth also became popular, with the arrival of Dubonnet and Cinzano in bottles and Martini and Cusenier in casks, which were then bottled in the Sheares Street warehouse.

In the early 1960s the company continued to expand its sales of wine with carefully chosen marketing to match the increased demand. Tactics such as the annual Remnant Sale were used to clear excess stock at reduced prices. Woodford Bourne drew on its advertising skills with leaflet drops to all parts of the city, especially at Christmas, promoting the bread-and-butter range of Brown Label Whiskey and Red Label Guinness as well as offering French and German wines, "to go with the turkey". Denis O'Driscoll ran the wine department in the Patrick Street shop with enthusiasm, organising frequent tastings and making knowledgeable recommendations for customers. A trade in altar wine was also developed over the years with the supply to the churches in Munster and sometimes further afield.

In 1960 the company held a wine tasting opportunity for its customers at its Sheares Street cellars, the success of which significantly changed the company's approach to the market.

The Lord Mayor of Cork, Alderman Gus Healy – 2nd from left – together with Directors Brodie, James and David Nicholson, seen at the opening of the "Festival of Wine", held in 1964 in the Sheares street cellars.

In 1964, four years later, the company held a "Festival of Wine" in its cellars. This widely publicised event occurred over several days with wines on show from several wine-producing countries. Wines and fine ports were made available for tasting, supported by experts in viniculture, with a prize for the champion taster. Supported by wine agents and shippers from abroad, the attendances were well beyond expectations and included existing and potential customers, and experts from the wine and hostelry trades. The significant rise in profits for 1964 to £14,141 [2005 €250,000] demonstrated to the management at Woodford Bourne, and to David Nicholson in particular, the potential of the developing market for table wines in Ireland. New customers were being added throughout Munster in new hotels, restaurants and the increasing number of self-service retail shops.

In 1961 David Nicholson was joined in the business by his younger brother, Brian who had completed a number of years training in a Hotel and Hospitality school abroad, having completed a degree course at Trinity College, Dublin. Brian Nicholson took up responsibility for the administrative side of the company. At this time, the company was receiving professional consultancy advice from Bernard Uniacke of accountants McGuinness Burns Griffin. He attended Board meetings over a period of several years giving invaluable advice while the company was experiencing accelerated growth.

Capitalising on the expertise in wine sourcing, retail skills developed over generations, and in the accelerating switch to self service, Woodford Bourne opened its first wine store 'Fine Wines' in the Cork suburb of Turners Cross, in 1964. The store was managed by John Morrissey and sold a wide variety of wine from France, Spain, Italy and Germany as well as spirits distributed or bottled by the company. The availability of parking, late opening and a relaxed service atmosphere within the store, ensured immediate success. Customers were provided with an opportunity to learn about the various wines and their countries of origin in the knowledge that they were choosing from a studied range backed by a long-standing Cork based business tradition.

Brian Nicholson, the author's brother and only other family director of the company for many years. His wise counsel was of particular importance as the group started to accelerate in the late 1960s and 1970s.

Retail success was mirrored by efforts to develop the wholesale drinks business. In 1962 Jerry Cashman was promoted from the warehouse to develop the wholesale business. He widened distribution in Munster and up the west coast with the product range of "house brands" and key products. Success came quickly, and in 1964 a second person was taken on. The company increased profitability continuing to widen its own portfolio of brands and to increase its market share whilst being able to lower distribution costs through increasing volumes.

Lionel Bruck, the proprietor of the well respected wine exporting company, Hasenklever, seen pointing out to the author some of the qualities he looked for in a young red Burgundy. A specialist in the finer wines of the Cote de Nuits vineyards in France, Lionel was known for his acumen in picking out winners.

One of the most important contracts secured by Jerry Cashman was the catering contract for Bunratty Castle in County Clare which was a landmark tourist destination popular with the growing number of tourists from the United States. The company took on the responsibility for supplying bulk wine for their extensive banqueting business, a contract that continued until 1988.

In keeping with the national move to establish better working conditions for staff, the Directors initiated a staff pension scheme. Proposed by James Frederick Nicholson, this was established with Irish Life Assurance company in October 1965. The conditions were that employees must have at least five years service with the company and be under the age of fifty five.[1] The scheme was non-contributory, with the option for members to join a voluntary one if preferred.

Jerry Cashman, the company's first wine and spirit salesman.

By the mid 1960s, it seemed that the country had left the depressing days of the 1950s. The new economic policies appeared to be having an effect as real output increased in Ireland by an average of 4.4% between 1960 and 1973. Increased investments in industry, agriculture and in the tourism sector were rapidly opening up new opportunities for the wholesaling trade. Product development and self-service retail distribution increased the sales of wines and spirits. Woodford Bourne met the challenges by extending its wines and spirits range. The successful wine festival in the Sheares Street cellars highlighted the latent interest in wine. At the same time greater quality control was achieved by wineries who bottled their own produce. Wine brands were developed with marketing support and gradually the successful wines received recognition, acceptance and market share.

CHAPTER 8

Wholesale and Retail Development

"Europa Cyprus Sherry opens the door"

The ten years beginning in 1965 was a significant period for the expansion and growth of Woodford Bourne. Building on the foundations laid in the previous ten years, the company made huge strides in the table wine market with the amplification of its product range while simultaneously developing its wholesale and retail wine distribution networks. The period saw significant expansion in the Irish economy, the joining of the Economic Community in 1973 and major changes in the market with the evolution of the hospitality industry and the continued growth of the self-service supermarkets. Developments in the family saw the fourth generation taking over, with the retirement of family members and the promotion of David Nicholson to the position of Managing Director in 1969.

Following on the success of its first wine store opened at Turners Cross in 1964, the company continued to develop its retail network in Cork city and county and in Limerick city, under the "Fine Wines" banner. Shops were opened in Bishopstown and Limerick (1967), Ballintemple (1968) and the Turners Cross store was moved to the growing suburb of Douglas on the outskirts of Cork city. Sales in the stores increased steadily, benefiting from the rapidly developing market for table wine and aided by the efforts of the distributors to educate the palates of their customers. From past experience Patrick Street shop sales were boosted by the use of mailshots, tastings and advertising in local papers. The expanding range of wines came from the main wine producing markets in France, Italy, Spain and Germany.

Self service – an innovation at the time – was introduced in all stores. Customers were encouraged to browse and choose wines for themselves. Well-trained sales staff greatly added to the effectiveness of the stores as customers sought and received advice on the newer wines. Of all the stores opened, Fine Wines in Roche's Street, Limerick under the management of Terry Connolly was the most profitable. This was achieved mainly due to his expertise and management style of giving advice and prompt delivery of purchases. Terry also cultivated customers amongst the city's commercial businesses and the company secured a significant amount of the corporate gift market in the city.

Opposite page: The first road tanker to arrive at the company's cellars, carrying the equivalent of 30,000 bottles. The various wines would then be pumped into the newly acquired holding tanks in the modernised bottling area of the Bonded warehouse. The quality having been checked, the bottling, labelling and packing would proceed.

In 1966, following on the increased investment in the wholesale business and the success of its operations in Munster, Woodford Bourne engaged in a new venture with the opening of its first Cash and Carry. Situated within the Sheares Street warehouse, it stocked spirits, a limited range of wines and some beers. This venture was designed to save the cost of servicing the catering establishments, and to accommodate the traders and publicans who were prepared to come directly to purchase for cash. The change in the mix of trade was immediately noticeable, with 29% of all the company's wine and spirit business coming from the cash and carry in 1969 – 1970.[1] Further outlets were opened in the main urban centres beginning with the opening of the Waterford depot in 1967. This was managed by Dan O'Neill whose enthusiasm and dynamic approach appealed to the Waterford publicans, with sales increasing quickly. The Limerick Cash and Carry was opened in 1971, followed by one in Harold's Cross in Dublin in 1972 and in Galway in 1974. Joe Horgan with his sincere and friendly manner took control of the Galway outlet.

In accomplishing this, Woodford Bourne were the first company in the wine and spirit business to operate a national Cash and Carry distribution network. The average size of each unit was 5,000 square feet, providing a healthy cash flow requiring small reinvestment. Openings were followed by aggressive marketing at competitive prices, especially of the brands owned by the company. The Cash and Carry volumes gave the company the opportunity to buy on keener terms a wide range of branded spirits, sherries and wines. Understandably, sales margins were very tight, with monthly spirits offers sometimes being sold near cost. The impact on overall gross margin was noticeable as it dropped from 17.5% in 1970 to 11.0% in 1972, reflecting the mix of low-margin Cash and Carry trading in the new substantially increased turnover. The overall low gross margin left little scope for overhead expenses, shortages or breakages. The large through-put of products in Sheares Street created its own problems with the requirement for extra storage space in Bond. A five-ton truck was purchased for delivery to the outlets; cash collection of "cash-on-delivery" (C.O.D.) needed re-organisation, as did the handling and security of large quantities of cash. But the company had substantially improved its profit levels, establishing itself nationally and taking a step ahead of the competition.

As Woodford Bourne grew geographically it was always on the lookout for new products and brands to add breadth and depth to its product range. In 1967 a significant breakthrough was made with its innovation in the sherry market which formally had been dominated by Spanish sherries, in particular Winters Tale, Celebration Cream and Tio Pepe. It appeared to David

Nicholson that Cyprus Sherry was a special opportunity; it was of excellent quality but of a preferential duty rate due to Cyprus's membership of the Commonwealth. Recognising the potential combined with the unique position of Woodford Bourne – with its warehousing, bottling capability and distribution network – Europa Cyprus Sherry was born.

Following trial marketing with potential customers in the Patrick Street store, the decision to develop the sherry for the Irish market was taken. It was launched in 1967 at the R.D.S, supported by a television and tasting campaign partly funded by the Cyprus exporters. Sold in a clear glass 40oz bottle under the registered brand Europa, it also featured an attractive specially designed label. The perception with the customers was value for money with a quality on a par with the Spanish sherries currently on the market. Three brands were sold; Europa Cream, Europa Pale and Europa Golden. The sherry was shipped in casks to Cork, but as sales increased, it was transported from a tank farm in England in road tankers, each containing 5,000 gallons. Replenishment from the tank farm was by ship direct from the exporters in Cyprus. The success of Europa was a major breakthrough for the company.

National distribution in the supermarkets and off licences enabled Woodford Bourne to look at the entire Irish market for the first time. In order to concentrate its efforts in the Dublin market, Gordon Hunter joined Woodford Bourne on a part-time basis. His efforts quickly resulted in increased sales and he succeeded in cementing the company's image with the trade. This was a carefully planned methodical approach with an appreciation of the difficulty any company based outside Dublin had in establishing itself in the Dublin market.

During this period the annual supplies of bulk whiskey to wholesalers by Irish Distillers ceased. This would eventually deny Woodford Bourne its traditional profitable market for Jameson's whiskey, which had been sold under the company's Brown Label brand since the 1890s.

The timing of the launch of Europa and Mirabeau, the company's two national brands, was perfect. It coincided with the demise in profitability available from Brown Label, which was due to the decision of Irish Distillers to terminate the supplies of bulk whiskey.

However, as the whiskey was stored by the company prior to bottling, stocks did not run out for another ten years, enabling the company to explore other avenues for growth. This move by Irish Distillers was the eventual death knell for many competitors who could not adapt to new trends and opportunities.

Joining the company in 1964, Ken Daunt was the driving force in the organisation of the first two Cash and Carrys. His enthusiasm and hard work knew no bounds, while he also had the leadership qualities to develop a keen team spirit with all involved in sales. After the opening of the Limerick Cash and Carry, in 1971, he diverted his attention to the Dublin market. A central warehouse in Harold's Cross was purchased and Frank Donegan joined the company from John Morgan and Sons to manage the Dublin Cash and Carry and develop sales. He guided a closely knit team who slowly but surely gained regular customers. They signed up the major Hotel groups, the busy night club venues in Leeson Street and expanded the off-license business. With his marketing expertise, Ken Daunt took on the responsibility for all the major supermarket retail accounts including Superquinn, Quinnsworth and H. Williams. A reliable and steady service was key to ensuring long term trading relationships with these companies. The sales staff had been increased substantially, with Frank Donegan controlling the Dublin market aided by Noel Tallant and Lena Kerrins who merchandised and organised tastings in the major Dublin supermarkets and Cash and Carrys.

Jerry Cashman was promoted to Sales Manager for Munster and Connaught. Over the years Jerry had consistently achieved excellent results while avoiding bad debts. He was ably supported by Noel Frawley, Dan O'Neill, Joe Horgan and Paddy Flynn who was appointed as the Woodford Bourne agent in the South East region.

A five gallon copper jug, which would have been one of the "work horses" in the cellars in the earlier days. Slightly dented through use, but otherwise in perfect condition.

Fast changing times brought opportunity, with new businesses opening and others closing. As the company obtained international brands so the services of advertising and public relations agents Adsell, run by Paddy Considine, were needed. Each new product had to be carefully launched in the market to maximise limited resources. The principles in general left this up to their agents, Woodford Bourne, usually with some outside guidance at an annual visit to discuss progress. A common feature of the time was the provision of marketing or promotional support by the supplier to part fund the advertising and promotion of the product in the Irish market. Brand and company awareness was furthered by sponsorship.

The opportunity to sponsor the Clarinbridge Oyster Festival was taken by Woodford Bourne as it sought to build on the efforts of Jerry Cashman as he continued to develop business in the western region where the company was by now very dominant. In the mid 1960s Woodford Bourne sponsored the main banquet of the Oyster Festival, achieving national exposure at a time when it was developing a presence in the Dublin market and extending its product range.

In 1967, in keeping with the approach of seeking new business opportunities, Woodford Bourne set up the Central Staff Agency (C.S.A.). Modelled on successful staff placement businesses then operating in London, the agency immediately filled a requirement in the Cork market. Following an advertisement in the Cork Examiner, Claire Hendrick was recruited to research the opportunity and set up the business. CSA was immediately a profitable success. Over the years this business grew with the establishment of branches in Limerick and Dublin (1977). The expansion into Dublin failed to achieve sufficient temporary or permanent placements and the operation there soon ceased trading. However the agency in Cork proved to be profitable without capital investment and was located above the retail shop, in existing premises owned by the company.

Press features were usually included in the launch of a new restaurant or wine shop. The company was proud to be involved, taking the opportunity to publicise its newly established chain of Cash and Carry depots.

Choicest of The Empire's Vintages
EMU BRAND AUSTRALIAN WINES

These Australian wines were available on the Irish market, from the early 1900s. The red Burgundy was bottled in flagons of slightly over a litre capacity and retailed for five shillings in 1925. Few other wines from Australia, were imported until the 1980s.

In 1968, Woodford Bourne further extended its geographic spread by purchasing a 24%[2] stake in Irish Vintners, a company recently formed by Williams Egan of Tullamore, W.H White of Limerick, John Fitzgerald of Tralee and Frank Searson of Dublin. The company was chaired by non-executive Tom Whelehan, the well regarded wine correspondent. Irish Vintners had, with the support of the shareholders (the member companies), a large sales force covering most of the on and off-license premises in the Republic. It was now able to offer major international wines and spirits brand owners a powerful service. Spirit brands included Teachers Scotch whisky, Pernod-Ricard Anis, Beefeater Gin, Southern Comfort, Bisquit Brandy and Cointreau. Wine brands included Taylors Port, Bollinger Champagne, Blue Nun, Antinori Italian wines, Sichel French wines and St Rafael Aperitif.

Irish Vintners was run as an independent business selling to the trade generally, as well as expecting special support from the member companies. The company's general manager promoted listed and new drinks to the member companies and all other wholesalers alike, while at same time a dedicated marketing professional sought to develop new channels and listings in the retail trade.

Brian Nicholson's son, Alan who runs the Central Staff Agency, founded in 1967. CSA was the first company in Cork to offer a staff recruitment service, specialising in the placement of permanent and temporary office staff at all levels.

This alliance with Irish Vintners gave Woodford Bourne a wider range of agency products which had slightly better margins and promotional material to help boost sales. This coincided with the growth of the hospitality and catering sectors, where wine sales were growing rapidly. Woodford Bourne's sales staff would make recommendations to hoteliers on their selection of wines and would supply attractive wine lists for their customers. Because of its expertise and knowledge of wine the company continued to prosper as many traditional wholesalers closed during the period due to a static and underdeveloped product range. As competition strengthened, Woodford Bourne were adept at drawing in promotional monies from their own agency suppliers. These funds were used to resource marketing and communications plans for the products concerned, increasingly on a national basis as the company grew. By 1970 Woodford Bourne was trading nationally with the exception of the North Midlands and the East coast north of Dublin.

Irish Vintner's portfolio of brands included a wide range of wine and spirit products, many of which are seen to this day on prominent display in most licensed outlets. The company achieved substantial success in increasing the sales of Teacher's Scotch Whisky and Pernod.

CHAPTER 9

Success Through New Products & Brands

"Passing the £1 Million mark"

Appointed as Managing Director in 1969, following 15 years with the company, David Nicholson recalls these times as follows:

"Titles were not important but I suppose the appointment signified that my father wanted to take it easy. The business was changing and it was my job to move it forward and of course I still had his wise counsel and advice. My brother Brian and I analysed the strengths and weaknesses, identified profitable sectors and assessed opportunities around them. We were in the grocery and wine and spirit trades and had to make decisions and I suppose my bias was to the wine area".

David's father, James Frederick Nicholson and uncle, Victor Brodie Nicholson both retired in the following year after long careers in the business. Both these resignations were accepted with regret, however their services as advisors and consultants were retained. Board Minutes of the time record the event: "Both Directors have given a lifetime of service to the company. Dating back over a period of political and economic uncertainty in this country they have directed the resources of the company in a careful and prudent way."[1] Records for the time show a sales level of £673,000 [2005 €9.0m] for the year 1970/1971 which rose to over the £1.0 million mark [2005 €12.3m] the following year. Profits for 1971/1972 were £123,000 [2005 €1.5m].

Recognising the potential of the market for table wine and encouraged by the success of the wine stores in Cork, the Patrick Street store was extensively remodelled. The grocery department, which had suffered trading difficulties, was closed and the extensive wine range moved to the front of the store near the busy street. This trend was mirrored in Dublin with the closure of the Findlater grocery outlets - another family business – a number of years later.

As the wine displays were extended, a flower shop was established at the western side of the store. This new business proved to be a profitable use of space until the introduction of a fast food outlet in 1980. At the same time the company tea tasting and blending room was

Opposite page: One of the six vineyards owned by the Torres family in Chile. A country that is a viticultural paradise, in part thanks to the remarkable absence of the Phylloxera virus, making it a sought after location by winemakers the world over. Miguel Torres recognised these virtues, establishing a winery in Curico in 1979.

converted into a most impressive board room, with timber panelling and suitable furnishings giving the room its unique atmosphere. The Managing Directors' new office on the second floor of the building commanded strategic views of Patrick Street and the Grand Parade. This had been for many years the residence of General Tom Barry, and his wife Leslie formerly chairman of the Red Cross.

The company invested in a faster, more automated bottling line and extra wine storage tanks in its Sheares Street warehouse. Although the trend towards bottling in the vineyards had been established since the 1950s, Woodford Bourne continued to enjoy advantages through the operation of its own line. The taxation policy of the time enabled the company to purchase quality product in bulk and deliver it for sale in bottles on the Irish market at a competitive price. This was of vital importance as customers sought to purchase new reasonably priced varieties of table wine, vermouth and whiskey. Eventually there were only three merchants in the country capable of a substantial bottling output; Woodford Bourne, Gilbeys and Grants of Ireland. However when this tax benefit was phased out some years later it reduced the benefits obtained by bottling in Ireland.

Continued development of its product portfolio was achieved through the aggressive search for new wine agencies. Encouraged by the success of Europa sherries, David Nicholson took on personal responsibility for the sourcing of new products overseas and forging new relationships. The lower priced volume segment of the table wine market was the next to be targeted as the company sought easily drinkable value-for-money table wines.

Opposite Page:
The author seen
checking the quality of
the latest shipment of
red and white wines
which had just been
bottled under the
company's brand
"Mirabeau". This
photo is taken in the
"wet" cellar
(see Chapter 4)
which some years
before would have
housed casks of
maturing whiskey.

Bulk red and white wine was obtained from the south of France; red from a supplier in Sete, and white from a co-operative in the region around Beziers. The bulk wine was transported to Ireland by road tanker and bottled in the Sheares Street warehouse in Cork. These light French table wines were launched in 1972, as Mirabeau , and were sold in 1 litre bottles and supported by a nationwide marketing campaign. The wine rapidly assumed the number two position in the market behind Hedges and Butler's Hirondelle, with sales at 25,000 bottles per month.

Success with this litre size was soon followed by an Italian wine of a similar standard. Bought from a family-owned company – Messrs. Pasqua of Verona. Valpolicella, Soave and Bardolino were all sold in magnum sized bottles with colourful eye catching labels. Along with Europa Cyprus Sherry and Mirabeau French wines, Pasqua's Italian Magnums gave the company a

third fast moving brand popular in the supermarket and off-licence sectors. Further products were added for the restaurant trade; Cepage D'Or, a range of French wines, and Weinfrau from Germany were both bottled abroad with exclusive labels for Woodford Bourne. Filapetti Vermouth, a competitively priced Italian aperitif, was also stocked as vermouth was a fashionable growth sector at the time.

The early 1970s also saw the sourcing and bottling of the lighter German wines Liebfraumilch, Oppenheimer, Niersteiner and Bernkastler from the Rhine and Moselle Valleys. The wines were mellow and very drinkable but they were difficult to transport due to their light alcohol content. To ensure stability the level of free sulphur had to be checked on arrival in each cask and topped up where necessary. Woodford Bourne developed a relationship with Louis Guntrum of Nierstein um Rhein to bottle these wines with special equipment and in strictly sterile conditions. By availing of the economies of Irish bottling, Guntrum was able to offer small quantities to the wholesale traders at competitive prices. In 1975 the company imported a range of wines from Weber of Trier. Bottled in West Germany, these wines were the first low priced German wines to be sold in the Irish market.

Since the 1960s the wine growers of the Beaujolais region in France had employed an innovative marketing technique to sell their wines. Beaujolais, a red wine from the Gamay wine stock is an "appellation controlee" region which produces a substantial amount of wine annually. Unlike most red wines, this wine does not need ageing in the bottle due to it being fermented by the carbonic semi-maceration process which gives a quicker evolution of taste. Beaujolais Nouveau was launched with considerable publicity by the media, and wine importers in Ireland and the UK competed each year to be the first to bring the new year's crop to the market in their respective countries. Woodford Bourne were the winners in 1971 with Beaujolais supplied by Messrs Jean Thorin, one of the longest established and largest companies in the Beaujolais region. This was a substantial cash flow bonus for the exporter with 30% of the crop sold immediately. Generally it was very drinkable, especially if the weather had been sunny immediately prior to picking the grapes.

Irene Margaret (Peggy Ronan), daughter of Arthur Edward Nicholson, with her brother Commander Vernon Nicholson O.B.E.

After an approach by a Cork businessman, Leslie Auchincloss, who had the recipe and the necessary permission to sell poteen, Ivernia Distillation Blenders was set up to compound and bottle this new product under Bond in Woodford Bourne's Sheares Street warehouse. While sales of "Secret Still" were difficult to establish in Ireland, it became a popular seller in stone crocks in the Duty Free shop in Shannon Airport. Following attendance at a Trade Fair in the USA, an agreement was reached with Fleischmans, a subsidiary of Standard Brands, to market and distribute the product in the USA. A special label was designed and a magnificent launch planned at the Inn on the Park in Central Park, New York. David writes: "It was a night to remember with many leading dignitaries in the drinks trade including regional distributors, wholesalers, large retailers and members of the company's staff from all parts of America, all wanting to meet "the man from Ireland". The highlight was leprechauns serving poteen with your favourite mixer while an Irish group played rebel songs including "The Men Behind the Wire"! After some initial success the resources and effort to promote the product in the American market were not forthcoming from the American agents and sales ground to a halt in 1977.

In 1973, Terry Connolly returned to Cork, from successfully managing the shop in Limerick, to the position of Group Buyer and Stock controller at the Sheares Street warehouse. After the steady growth of the company and the development of the distribution systems for the "Fine Wines" retail and Cash and Carry outlets, the company was under severe pressure to maintain service levels for all the businesses. Terry provided the discipline and organisation to control the growing demand. With the expanded business it was now economical to ship from all the leading suppliers in container loads of 800 cases. And with the flexibility of being able to send the ten-ton-truck to pick up mixed loads from various French suppliers, the company was able to widen its range and maximise cash flows. Prices would be negotiated at the beginning of the year with reserves for major suppliers being placed for the

This label was specially designed for the American market. Note the spelling of "Potcheen", the Irish authorities permitted wording for the product.

Dan O'Neill, a member of the Woodford Bourne sales staff, spent two months in the Boston area to back up the American distributors sales launch.

same period. Credit at 90 days was the norm, with a number of suppliers giving 180 days with a 3% surcharge on any period over the normal 90 days. Products were paid for by Bills of Exchange; some suppliers waived these based on their trust in the Woodford Bourne name.

As Woodford Bourne expanded and became more diverse, the directors decided it was time to seek outside professional support. The company developed a relationship with the Irish Productivity Council (IPC), a government subsidised body who specialised in advising and supporting growing companies. Following a review of its operations, the company installed a computer to manage the extensive product range, control the stocks throughout the business and manage the profitability of the company. With the success of this project, ongoing contact was established with one of the IPC senior consultants, Louis Kilmartin, whose guidance and advice was to contribute greatly to the advancement of the business in the years ahead. In 1974, the company split the property and trading arms of the business, with the property portfolio being transferred to Lee Vale Holdings and with trading put through Woodford Bourne and Co Ltd. This immediately gave greater transparency to the results as all properties were rented to the trading company. This enabled the owners to better identify the true profit areas in the business and earmark these for expansion and further investment.

In 1975, following market research and analysis of Spanish wines, Woodford Bourne secured the agency for the already internationally respected Spanish producer Miguel Torres. The company already sold some Rioja Spanish wine through its shops under the San Millan brand. A family company, Torres was one of the foremost producers of top-quality table wines in Spain. With brands such as Sangre de Toro, Vina Sol and Coronas, Woodford Bourne had a premier Spanish label to add to its list for national distribution. This coincided well with the large numbers of Irish holiday makers now visiting Spain and the Canary Islands where such wines were readily available. Having achieved a foothold in the Dublin market, one of the primary aims of the company on securing the agency was to have the Torres brand listed on all the leading restaurant wine lists in the capital.

The relationship with Torres was developed over time, but was not without its hurdles. On one occasion when David Nicholson was visiting the head office of Torres, in the Penedes region near Barcelona to discuss market progress he was welcomed by the Managing Director, the ageing Senor Torres. Waiving the visitor from Ireland to a seat he continued with his telephone conversation for some time. On finishing his call the phone immediately rang again and he commenced a further conversation. On seeing this David got up, gathered

his papers and stood up saying "Sr Torres, I have come from Ireland specially to discuss the marketing plans for your product and as you do not have the time to talk to me I am going home!" Immediately the phone went down and his hand came out. A bridge had now been crossed, extra promotion money was forthcoming and a long lasting relationship established.

Success came quickly through a thoughtful public relations campaign. Careful positioning of the range, supported by public relations, press visits to the producers' cellars and other carefully orchestrated marketing, in co-operation with the Torres family, cemented a solid public awareness and acceptance with wine drinkers. From annual imports in 1975 of around 200 cases the success of the Torres brand grew into a business selling nearly 20,000 cases a year by the mid 1980's. The Torres brand is still the number one Spanish quality wine brand in Ireland.

A selection of the popular Torres wines from Spanish and Chilean vineyards. Santa Digna Sauvignon Blanc (a favourite of the author's), has an opulent bouquet reminiscent of ripe tropical fruit. The palate is silvery and intense with a dry crispness.

The Company's sales staff seen on an educational visit to the Torres cellars and vineyards. Included from left are; Paddy Flynn (Waterford), Pat Bradley (Fine Wines, Douglas), Dan O'Neill (Waterford & later Kerry), Noel Frawley (Cork City and County), Joe Horgan (Galway), Ken Daunt (Woodford Bourne) and Lena Kerrins (Dublin).

In keeping with Woodford Bourne's policy to forge strong relationships with its suppliers as well as educating and developing its staff, a number of visits to leading producers in France and Germany were organised. Representatives from the company visited Hennessy, Bisquit Cognac and Donatian Bahaud in the Loire Valley. The following year Hasenklever, Thorin and Mommessin were visited in the Burgundy area. A particular highlight was an attendance by a team from Woodford Bourne at the annual Chevalier du Tastevin banquet held that year in Morey St Denis, France. Also, the wineries of Torres in Spain were visited by staff and customers on numerous occasions as relationships between the two companies developed. These visits were an important factor in fostering a strong team spirit and enthusiasm amongst the representatives of what was by then a rapidly growing company.

By the mid 1970s the company was passing approximately 120,000 cases of wine annually through its warehouse, capturing a major share of the growing market for table wines. The company had grown from a turnover of £500,000 in 1969 to £4,600,000 million by 1976

[2005 €30m], passing the £1,000,000 turnover mark in 1972. About seventy people were employed, with thirty involved in the direct selling of wine. Woodford Bourne had successfully launched and developed a number of new products, the most successful being Europa sherries and Mirabeau bulk table wines. However the ending of the tax advantage enjoyed by bottlers, in effect opened the market to any trader to import in containers any wines bottled at source.

With part of the benefit of Irish bottling eradicated, the company lost some of its price advantage, and access to established networks such as supermarkets, in what was rapidly becoming a commodity business. Finally the company had to face this challenge against the background of a worsening economic environment following the oil price shocks in 1973; the deteriorating fiscal situation as the budget deficit climbed to 6.8% of GDP by 1975; and an average inflation rate of 9.25% over the previous ten years. Added to the adverse economic climate the political situation in Northern Ireland was extremely volatile, severely damaging the tourism industry which had been partly responsible for the growth of the business.

CHAPTER 10

A New Business Priority

Investment in the Pub and Restaurant Sector

*J*ames Frederick Nicholson died in 1976. He had achieved over fourty years service with the company, many of them as Managing Director. He joined the company at a time of considerable unrest amongst the owners and had done much to negotiate a new ownership structure ensuring the continued stability of the company. During his tenure as Managing Director the company had expanded out of its traditional base into retailing and cash and carry wholesaling and had begun energetically to develop its table wine business. He was always patient and supportive of new suggestions provided they were calmly and carefully thought through. He cared for all staff and industrial unrest was unknown in the company. Many staff members were the relatives of previous generations of employees. As already indicated, one of his last actions was to set up a non-contributory pension scheme for all permanent staff. He lived to see such an unimaginable amount of cash moving through the books of account that he was amazed and slightly mesmerised!

During the late 1970s, the company developed its wine agency business following from the success of the Torres agency. In 1976 it was appointed the agent in the Irish market for Codorniu cava (sparkling wine) from Spain. This family company, founded in 1551, is based in Catalonia and was the largest producer of sparkling wine, with 15km of wine cellars containing 100 million bottles. The Codorniu cava was launched successfully into the Irish market where it quickly established itself as the product of choice in nightclubs because of its quality, and its substantial price advantage over traditional champagne brands. The Codorniu brand complemented the existing French sparkling wine Veuve de Verney and Boizel Champagne, both distributed by Woodford Bourne. A few years later, in 1980, the Codorniu company, recognising the sustained growth of their products in Ireland, nominated Woodford Bourne as their most successful distributor worldwide. This honour was very much appreciated as due to a very high duty on sparkling wines in Ireland, the product had been difficult to market successfully.

Opposite page:

Competitors in the Rabel Boat Race under sail down the Douro River, in Portugal. Organised annually by the Confraria do Vinho do Porto (Port Wine Brotherhood), the picture shows the Rabelos of Taylors which was distributed by Woodford Bourne. In ages past, Port wine was transported from the Douro vineyards to the wine lodges in Villa Nova de Gaia in these boats.

To the extensive distribution and growing market for table wines, Woodford Bourne added to their wine list another successful Spanish exporter, Julian Chivite, from the Navarra region and three highly respected French exporters: Donatien Bahaud from the Loire valley; Jean Pierre Brotte from the Rhone valley; Jean Thorin from the Burgundy region. The company of Jean Pierre Brotte was especially known for the quality of their Chateau Neuf du Pape, a rich full bodied red wine. But price increases from the company were a constant problem for Terry Connolly. On one occasion, following a request for a further increase, he visited the vineyards in Chateau Neuf du Pape. After a meeting with the representatives of the company, all went to watch the local rugby team who were playing that day and won their match. Needless to say, the demand for a price increase was dropped for that year!

Woodford Bourne also recognised the opportunity for the sale of New World wines both for their quality and marketing approach. Being labelled with the names of the grapes from which they were grown, they were more easily recognisable by the consumer; Chardonnay, Sauvignon Blanc and Chenin Blanc for white grapes and Cabernet Sauvignon, Merlot and Shiraz for red. New World wine was sourced from Torres who had planted vineyards in Curico, Chile, some years previously. Miguel Torres, a highly qualified viticulturalist, made the most of the very suitable local conditions for producing crisp aromatic wines from the Sauvignon Blanc grape while Cabernet Sauvignon was planted to produce a full bodied fruity red wine. Woodford Bourne was also honoured to take on the agency for Robert Mondavi from the Napa Valley, in California. Wines from Mondavi were very highly regarded in the U.S.A. and were very acceptable to the top restaurants in Ireland. Brown Brothers, one of the oldest established vineyards in Victoria, Australia, and still a family business, also offered their wines to Woodford Bourne. Theirs was a quality product with some interesting varietals including Dry Muscat, an un-wooded white wine with enticing fresh flavours. This focus on successful and established exporters of fine wines enabled Woodford Bourne to present a formidable selection to the increasingly educated and discriminating trade buyers.

Celebrating with Codorniu, the leading producer of Cava sparkling Spanish wine, made using the method champenoise.

A proud moment for Woodford Bourne. The presentation of the 1980 International Export Trophy as the most successful distributor of Codorniu globally in that year. Pictured at the celebration lunch in Dublin were, from left:

Don Manuel Raventos, head of the House of Codorniu;

Juan Cros, Financial Director of Codorniu;

Ken Daunt, Managing Director of Woodford Bourne;

David Nicholson, Chairman of Woodford Bourne

and

M.J. Millour, Codorniu Export Director.

In order to create more awareness of the company Woodford Bourne in the trade, more exposure to the media was needed in Dublin. It was decided to sponsor the Woodford Bourne golf trophy with the support of the Irish Golf Association. A four ball was staged in every golf club in Dublin on New Years Day with the winners going forward to represent their clubs in the play-off at selected clubs and the competition reached an annual climax at a selected golf course. The venues were Elm Park (1976), Woodbrook (1977), Forest Little (1978), Edmondstown (1979) and Newlands (1980).

As part of creating greater awareness both for Woodford Bourne and its brands, this period also saw the launch of the Woodford Bourne Wine Awards. Launched in conjunction with Hotel and Catering Review, the awards were specifically aimed at the catering and hospitality industry with the intention of supporting the restaurant business. Open to all establishments that served wine with meals, the criteria included the presentation of wines, introduction of wine to the customer, the design and layout of the wine list and innovations in promotion. The adjudication panel consisted of members from the Irish Hotel and Catering Institute, the Irish Restaurant Owners Association, the Irish Hotels Federation and the Wine Promotion Board. The winning group enjoyed a busy weekend being feted in a European vineyard.

Building on the popularity of Europa and Mirabeau the company had consistently developed its range as has been shown with the addition of high profile names such as Torres, Codorniu, Robert Mondavi and Brown Brothers. With a declared intention to target the best restaurants and hotels in the country, Woodford Bourne had built up a business in a growing market where consumer tastes were still developing. Woodford Bourne had now become the second largest wine distributor in the country with a wide range of popular products that covered the off-licences and supermarkets as well as the Hotel and Restaurant trade. A highly motivated and committed sales staff of thirteen supported by merchandisers kept progress moving forward. Although Gilbey's were still clearly the leader with approximately 30% of the market for wines in Ireland, Woodford Bourne had worked its way up to hold 18%, in what was still a fragmented industry. Analyses show that the company was reliant on the success of three key lines for a substantial contribution to profits; Mirabeau was the top contributor with Pasqua second and Europa third.

Following on the success of the Oyster Tavern, the company extended its operations into pubs and restaurants, allowing it to diversify from its base in wholesaling into retail markets. In 1974 the shop premises of John Rearden and Sons, on Washington Street, was purchased. The Directors at the time were considering the redevelopment of the Patrick Street premises. When this idea was discarded, Rearden's shop was converted into a rustic cellar bar with a buffet style luncheon which immediately proved popular with business and legal clientele. Run very efficiently by Dermot O'Morchoe, the pub traded successfully for a number of years and annually hosted the Cork Oyster Festival. Some years later, in 1984, having reached an optimum level of turnover, the Board sold the pub to capitalise on the very substantial profit available on the investment.

By 1978, the company also decided to develop the space behind its Patrick Street shop premises, opening Carnabys pub with live music entertainment. The pub was full when music was hosted by a leading entertainer, but almost empty otherwise. After a short period the doors were closed and the company rethought its use for the premises. After research and analysis of emerging national pub trends, the premises was remodelled in a style from the early 1920s which created a relaxed atmosphere and was launched as Maguires Pennyfarthing Inn.

Reardens Cellar Bar hosted the Cork Oyster Festival for several years, in the late 1970s and early 1980s. At the announcement of the oyster opening competition were, from left: Dermot O'Morchoe, Manager of Reardens; Michael Long, Managing Director, Murphy's Brewery. Tom McKiernan, Public Relations Officer, Woodford Bourne; David Hugh-Jones, Oyster Grower & Sponsor.

The manager at the outset was Dan Cronin, followed by Dan O'Brien who between them set high standards. Later the dedicated Charlie Meeghan took over with the venue quickly establishing itself as one of the busiest pubs in the city.

At a board meeting in the late 1970s it was agreed to look for further sites for the development of public houses. The first site obtained was in Grange near the village of Douglas. Although detailed plans were drawn up and planning permission obtained, the plans were shelved due to the requirement for cash and energy elsewhere in the business. This property was eventually sold at a considerable profit. During this time Woodford Bourne was developing its management expertise in the pub business, since both the management recognised the importance of this trade in the future.

A further development took place in 1983 when the Mardyke Snooker Club was established in the old wine warehouse in Sheares Street. The club was designed to respond to market changes and the increased exposure of snooker on television; the venue was equipped with twelve full-sized tables installed on the first floor. Surplus space was now available upstairs as smaller stocks were being held due to the importation of wines in bottle. The business was quick to take off, and a further thirty three snooker tables as well as eight ten pin bowling lanes, pool tables, videos and a snack bar were added.

With the continued investment in new products and the reliance on the extensive retail and cash and carry distribution systems the company began to experience overtrading in the late 1970s, with increasing demands for the cash generated by the company. The economic climate had worsened considerably since the good years of the early 1970s. Unemployment rose and the average inflation rate was 13.5% for the eleven years 1975 to 1985. Simultaneously the government progressively increased the duty on wines and spirits, as it sought to fund its fiscal expansion of the late 1970s and early 1980s. In the company pressure on gross margins was growing with a simultaneous increase in debtors and bad debts. In 1978, prompted by these trends and the increasingly competitive environment, especially from "one-stop" shopping, the company again commissioned the Irish Productivity Centre (IPC) to analyse its various operations and recommend courses of action. Of particular concern at the time was the inability of the company to invest in the growing pub business due to the working capital constraints of the trading company.

Two of the popular wines from Brown Brother's, Victoria, Australia. Pictured are the Dry Muscat and Shiraz.

Others included Merlot, Chardonnay, Orange Muscat and Flora, Late harvested Riesling and dessert wines. Brown Brothers, still a family company, celebrated one hundred years of winemaking, in 1979. Research into new grape varieties and blends continues to this day.

The report from IPC recommended a rationalisation of the company's operations to reduce its working capital requirements. Examination of the Cash and Carry business found control weaknesses and poor systems which were contributing to cash flow problems. IPC produced a plan to radically improve this situation. This resulted in the closure of the Cash and Carry outlets in Waterford, Limerick and Galway, with the distribution to affected customers being undertaken from the warehouses in Cork and Dublin. The recommendations also concluded that sales of non-company controlled spirits should be discontinued and that the transport system should be reorganised.

Jean Pierre Brotte, proprietor of the export house Brotte Le Clos in Chateau neuf-du-Pape, France, chats with Ken Daunt. Brottier, their brand of Cote de Rhone and handled by Woodford Bourne was at the time the largest selling Cote de Rhone on the Irish Market.

These measures, combined with a strict control of debtors and the introduction of an incentive-based cash plan for sales staff, went a considerable way to correcting the situation. In the event this action was timely; by 1981 interest rates on commercial loans had risen to 23.5%.

In 1980, Ken Daunt was appointed Managing Director, with David Nicholson assuming the role of Chairman. This was the first time a non-family-member had been appointed as Managing Director of the company, always a milestone in a family business. Since joining Woodford Bourne in 1964, Ken had been at the forefront of many of the commercial developments, and had played a key role in dealing with the multiple retailers such as Quinnsworth and Dunnes Stores. At the same time, the board was strengthened by the appointment of Hugh Duffy who became Finance Director; Frank Donegan was appointed Marketing Director and Terry Connolly became Purchasing and Operations Director.

In a further adjustment to its product range, the source for Europa sherry was changed from Cyprus to England. James Mather and Son based in Leeds was chosen, with whom Woodford Bourne was to develop a very profitable relationship. The earlier advantage of buying the sherry from Cyprus in bulk ended as duty rates for the area were brought into harmony with those in the European Union (EU) with the addition of a "Non EC Wines" import levy. Importing from Britain in bottle ensured lower stocks, greater cash flows and the maintenance of margins without raising prices. Mather's undertook to hold their prices constant over a period of two years which was especially helpful, given the high inflation of the time. The Europa brand name was retained with the result that the volumes only decreased by 10% as the majority of customers were happy with the quality of this new source. The level of gross profits of the Europa brand was particularly important for the wholesale company against the background of difficult trading conditions generally.

The growth in the national trade for cider was noted by the management team who recognised an opportunity to compete with the Bulmers cider brand. Ken Daunt approached Tauntons Cider in the UK, reached an agreement and a marketing plan was drawn up. Initially the Dry Blackthorn brand was imported for the off sales market and its introduction was supported by a limited television campaign. Prominent exposure was obtained in the supermarkets with the achievement of an acceptable consumer response. After good growth in off-licence sales, Woodford Bourne was also appointed the agent for draft sales in Munster. However despite an aggressive market entry strategy, which included fitting dispensers to public houses, the sales of draft cider did not reach the expectations of Tauntons, largely due to the dominating place already held by Bulmers. Eventually Taunton's confined their products on offer to Ireland to the supermarket and off-licence trade.

Coinciding with the cider venture, another product introduced was Konig Pilsner lager from Germany. Brewed by a long established company, the product was aimed at the premium end of the bottled lager market. Woodford Bourne decided to handle the distribution to the pub trade and off-licenses. Launched possibly without enough thought, it was only reasonably successful. In retrospect, a better strategy may have been to harness the established support of the regional beer companies, backing up the distribution with a national marketing plan.

During this period, to the end of the 1970s, Woodford Bourne consistently researched new products as a way of maintaining the growth which had accelerated at pace since the late 1960s. The rapidly changing market brought new opportunities which Woodford Bourne did its best to meet. On a visit to wine suppliers in Italy, David took time off to investigate the pasta market. However this idea died a death when sample cases en route from Italy, split open at Heathrow leaving trails of pasta dancing a jig on the carousel and a lost product opportunity. Not all product ideas were destined to make it to market!

CHAPTER 11

A Difficult Trading Environment

The Fifth Generation

Baileys Irish cream was launched in the late 1970s by W & A Gilbey's of Dublin. It was a new type of drink targeted at a relatively untapped sector of the market, the female drinker. The product was an instant success and sales of this liqueur seemed just about to explode world-wide with Baileys very much the market leader. David remembers the opportunity:

"After tasting, I realised that this new drink had a wide international potential. This could be a hugely exciting opportunity for us but immediate action was imperative."

After discussions with Brian Nicholson, a small dairy in Cork was approached but following an abortive start which set the project back six months, Woodford Bourne teamed up with the Mitchelstown Co-Operative. It was agreed that the Mitchelstown Co-Operative, would take a 30% share of the capital and would provide two nominees on the board along with David and Brian Nicholson, Ken Daunt and Terry Connolly.

Product development and test marketing took place over the next year which culminated in the launch and distribution of Royal Tara cream liqueur. Ken Daunt took charge and licensed the brand to a number of Woodford Bourne's prominent wine suppliers to distribute in a number of European countries. United Rum Merchants, the owners and distributors of Tia Maria were appointed to develop the market in the UK, Australia, South Africa and the Far East where they already had established sales organisations.

Sales were successfully established in the UK, France, Spain, Germany, Australia and Israel with exports to 25 countries within the first year of trading and a volume of 35,000 cases. Royal Tara became known for its quality and its hint of orange flavour that gave it an added extra appeal. The company was proud to win a Gold Medal at an International Fair in Amsterdam in 1982.

Opposite page: Royal Tara Irish Cream Liqueur wins a Gold Medal for Quality. David Nicholson seen here receiving the award in Amsterdam.

Difficulties began to surface as the success of the product became apparent. The Mitchelstown Co-Operative members began to question the partnership while at the same time quality issues were coming to light as the volumes increased. As the international market spread, the question of extending it to the large North American market was mooted. With the memory of the unsuccessful launch of Potcheen ten years previously, and realising the scale of investment required to successfully launch a product in so large and competitive a market, Woodford Bourne sold its share in the company to the Mitchelstown Co-Operative in 1983. This decision was taken after much thought and soul-searching as it seemed that the opportunity that faced the company was undoubtedly the greatest in its history, with considerable export market potential. However, as it later turned out, it was the correct decision as the brand was discontinued by the Mitchelstown Co-Operative some time later.

With the continuation of the difficult economic environment, Woodford Bourne continually looked for ways to reduce costs in its business. Once again a deep analysis was carried out by the two senior family Directors assisted by the Finance Director, Hugh Duffy. The strengths and weaknesses, opportunities and threats and product profitability were all assessed. In particular the ongoing cash flow management of the company was analysed. As already mentioned, in 1980 Woodford Bourne had taken the decision to discontinue stocking all non-Woodford Bourne spirit brands from its two remaining Cash and Carry outlets in Cork and Dublin. Competition in the sector coupled with the ongoing need to reduce its working capital requirements meant that it was no longer economical to hold large quantities of branded spirits.

In a further effort to reduce costs and complexity, the company ceased its association and profitable relationship with the other wholesalers in the Irish Vintners company. Membership of Irish Vintners Ltd. (IVL) had been causing difficulties for some time as competition with other Irish Vintners Limited company's sales forces selling the same brands caused diminished enthusiasm with Woodford Bourne's staff. Also there was some conflict of interest between the agency brands distributed by Woodford Bourne and those of Irish Vintners Limited. Consequently, Woodford Bourne decided, in the best interests of all, to sell their share of the IVL company in 1980, while simultaneously taking over the distribution rights for three key brands: Bollinger (Champagne), Taylors (Port), and San Rafael (French Aperitif).

From analyses of a number of industries and markets, one new growth area appealed to the Board. Fast food and particularly burgers were the exciting growth segment of the time. Indeed, some time earlier David had contacted McDonalds after a trip to the USA, to enquire about development possibilities in the Irish market only to discover that he was six months too late to acquire the master franchise.

The major fast food franchise possibilities at the time, therefore, were limited to Wendy's and Burger King. Both were approached and, after discussion, Woodford Bourne was offered the Irish franchise for Burger King but with a stipulation that the first unit had to be opened in Dublin with an additional unit annually thereafter. This did not suit the company who had identified the Patrick Street site as a prime one and the offer was rejected as the location of a successful franchise in such a high footfall location would provide the ideal solution to the future of the property. Wendy's were not ready for a launch in Ireland having not yet crossed the Atlantic. Failing to gain a franchise partner, Woodford Bourne decided to open on the Patrick Street site under their own name, Mandy's. A firm of consultants from London were appointed to advise on layouts, systems and controls. Plans were drawn up for the reorganisation of the premises and the planning permissions obtained. The Board estimated an initial investment of IR£100,000[1], and first year sales of IR£300,000 [2005 €1.2m].

Nigel Leeming, a manager working with the catering consultants in Britain with experience in the sector, was appointed manager and the first Mandy's outlet was opened in 1980. The initial launch and subsequent success of the Cork store was encouraging. A plan for further units was put together and a fine site in the main street of Leeds was virtually acquired but a last minute objection put paid to this project, due to open in 1981. The next opportunity was in Dublin but the choice of too small a site in O'Connells street meant the restaurant encountered difficulties competing with the established McDonalds franchise. This was an expensive mistake as turnover was not sufficient to cover the high fixed overheads. The company struggled but mounting losses pointed to a sale of the premises which was luckily achieved quickly in 1984.

Photograph taken outside of the main entrance to no. 64 Patrick Street which at the time housed the Mandy's fast food restaurant, with Gillian Harris in the foreground. The antique bicycle from Maguire's Pennyfarthing Inn is seen here been ridden by Francis O'Mahony on the occasion of the sponsorship of a local bicycle race by Mandy's.

Economic conditions and increasing competition in the group supermarket sector put continued pressure on margins. Innovation and investment in new avenues for growth resulted in disappointing results. New brand development, the investment in new pubs and forays into the fast food sector all demanded capital which had to come from retained earnings, as interest rates on commercial loans were prohibitive at the time. This was evident nationally in the severe deceleration in private sector investment which had fallen by 25% in real terms between 1979 and 1982. Company sales for 1982 of IR£5.9 million [2005 €17m] yielded a profit of IR£67,000 [2005 €190,000] or 1.1%. The company recorded a loss in the following year of IR£233,000 [2005 €600,000], the first since 1936, on static sales despite the high price inflation of the time.

Two years later, in 1985, the company's Finance Director Hugh Duffy, along with virtually the entire Dublin sales force, including the Marketing Director Frank Donegan, handed in their notice in a move to set up a wine business on their own in Dublin. This move was probably brought about by uncertainty in the company about the future of the wholesale business. In attempting to deal with this undoubted setback the company came to an agreement with those leaving to handle their agency products in the Dublin area. This arrangement worked reasonably successfully but it did leave its mark throughout the company.

1985 also saw positive developments, with the involvement of the fifth generation of the family in the business. Both Edward David Nicholson (son of James David Nicholson) and Alan Brian Nicholson (son of Brian McCowen Nicholson) joined the business with Alan taking responsibility for the CSA recruitment agency and Edward taking on the management of the Mardyke Snooker Club in the old Sheares Street warehouse. The developing competitive environment coupled with the continuing economic difficulties at home meant the company had to consider the future very carefully. Decisions would have to be taken about the long term prospects of the wholesaling business in comparison with the opportunities presented by the hospitality and pub sectors.

Picture taken in Maguire's Pennyfarthing Inn at the launch of new facilities, including a children's play area, at the Mardyke Leisure Complex in Sheares Street. From left: Jim O'Leary (Mardyke), David Nicholson, The Lord Mayor of Cork, Alderman Danny Wallace, Moira O'Hare (Mardyke) and Edward Nicholson.

CHAPTER 12

A Family Settlement

Consolidation, Sale and Aftermath

*I*n the light of the market changes, trading conditions and strategic options open to the business, the Directors commissioned the IPC to carry out a third strategic review of the business. Reporting back to the board in 1985, the findings provoked much thought and discussion amongst the family members. Confidence in business generally was at a low ebb in Cork with the closure of three of the largest trading concerns in the city and with a resulting increase in unemployment. By the mid 1980s unemployment nationally had reached a level of 14%, more than double the figure of a decade earlier.

The business itself had just passed through difficult trading conditions with high inflation and interest rates. Figures for 1985 show total sales of IR£7.34 million [2005 €16.7m] with 68% of these sales attributable to the wholesale wine business. Profits at IR£164,000 [2005 €375,000] represented 2.2% of sales. Critically, the report highlighted the general lack of growth expected in the wine market until at least the early 1990s. The high cost of bank finance further eroded the ability of private companies in this sector to make a profit.

The IPC report outlined the various businesses of the company as follows:

Wholesale wine distribution	(Woodford Bourne and Co. Ltd.),
Three Retail wine shops	(Fine Wines),
A bar business in Cork	(Maguire's Pennyfarthing Inn),
Two Fast Food outlets	(Mandy's),
One Fine Food restaurant	(The Oyster Tavern),
Staff recruitment and placement service	(C.S.A.),

Opposite page:
The Mardyke in 2005, an exciting leisure complex with a modern design, incorporated into the building of the old wine warehouse.

The warehouse, completed in 1875, is a listed building.

On the positive side there was good growth forecast in wine sales at some stage as Ireland at the time was drinking less table wine per capita than any other country in Europe. Wine sales had more than doubled since the early 1970s to 1.3 million cases a year, with over 90% of this volume made up of table wines. The directors were aware that Woodford Bourne would get a portion of this upswing with the portfolio of local and international brands built up over many years. However the company was vulnerable to the larger supermarket groups who could buy and import direct from source, as was the situation in the larger UK market.

The fifth generation of the Nicholson Family, Edward (known as Eddie). Since taking over control of the Mardyke, he has transformed the business by licensing the premises for a wider clientele.

Having begun trading in the bar and restaurant sector in the 1940s with considerable addition to the business since the 1970s, Woodford Bourne was well developed and was showing good return in trading and capital values. This approach also had the added benefit of investment in valuable city-centre property assets, which complemented the existing property portfolio of the company.

As well as recommending the rationalisation of a number of businesses in its report, the IPC also advised that the company further build up its asset base in the related food and drinks areas. The company had sold its interest in Reardens pub in 1984 due to constraints on expansion at the site. Following the IPC recommendation, David Nicholson had begun to search for new businesses with growth potential.

Both branches of the Nicholson family assessed their situation and with frank discussion sought clear and positive courses of action. Brian decided that, due to other commitments, he did not want to be involved in business any longer. David, however, wanted to continue but to consolidate through rationalisation. It gradually became clear that the wholesale operation would have to be sold in order for the two families to go their separate ways, while holding on to the asset portfolio. Finally the timing appeared to be appropriate with the arrival of the 5th generation as David and Brian's sons established themselves within the company.

Wanting to sell and actually selling are two very different propositions especially in a difficult trading environment. It was to take almost two years to eventually find a willing buyer. Discussions with two major groups were long but fruitless. It was through a series of cold calls that Ken Peare, the Managing Director of Wardell Roberts (now Robt. Roberts), took an interest. Wardell Roberts had a strong history in the Irish food & drink industry and had the financial resources and acumen to take a serious approach to the acquisition of Woodford Bourne. Talks resumed and in 1988 the wholesale business of Woodford Bourne and Co. Ltd. was sold with the transfer of the many fine wine agencies to Wardell Roberts. These agencies represented generations of work in sourcing, the development of relationships and the drawing up and implementation of joint marketing plans to launch the wines on the Irish market. In addition the company owned a number of wines bottled under license in France and Germany – Fillette, Cepage D'Or, Vin de Maison and the registered brands Europa and Mirabeau.

List of Agencies owned by Woodford Bourne in 1988

Agency	Area/Product	Country
Aurelien Grenouilleau	Bordeaux	France
Miguel Torres	Catalonia	Spain and Chile
Julian Chivite	Navarra	Spain
Bollinger S.A.	Champagne	France
Bodegas Sarda S.A.	Tarragona	Spain
Robert Mondavi Winery	California	USA.
Laurent Charles Brotte	Rhone	France
Thorin S.A.	Burgundy	France
Donatien Bahuaud&Cie	Loire	France
Fratelli Pasqua S.p.a	Veneto	Italy
S.A. des Eaux	Evian	France
Distilleri Riunite	Galliano Liqueur	Italy
Castillon Renault S.A.	Cognac	France
Duff Gordon & Co.	Sherry	Spain
J.E. Mather and Sons	Wine producers	UK
Taylor Fladgate & Yeatman	Port	Portugal
Brown Brothers	Victoria	Australia
Stones	Ginger Wine	U.K.

David writes: "For me this was a very difficult decision. I was the fourth generation of the Nicholson family in Woodford Bourne and I was at the fore-front in developing the wholesale wine trade and had many close contacts with suppliers abroad as well as the management and staff in the business. I dearly wanted to retain the name but this was obviously not realistic as we were selling the goodwill and agencies. We were to some extent pioneers in the new wave of development of the wine trade, making contacts abroad, building brands and educating and developing tastes. For me our success was very rewarding and satisfying. But it was time to move on and reorganise."

"Acquiring Woodford Bourne was quite a development in our corporate strategy," said Ken Peare, Chief Executive Officer, Robt. Roberts. "It was our first entry into the wines & spirits industry and at a time when this sector was suffering the effects of the economic downfall. However we were confident that the long history of the company and the fine range of wines in the portfolio, combined with the market know-how of Robt. Roberts could turn around the fortunes of Woodford Bourne."

Ken Peare, Chief Executive Officer of Woodford Bourne since 1988.

Upon the purchase of the business, Wardell Roberts transferred the distribution and marketing to its offices in Dublin. A number of years later the company was purchased by DCC, the publicly quoted company headed by Jim Flavin. The company continues to trade in Dublin to this day under the name Woodford Bourne Ltd. A brand new 18,000 square foot warehouse was opened in 2003 with a capacity to handle 100,000 cases of wines and spirits. Growth has been achieved through the development of new brands and the extension of sourcing to new countries of origin. Woodford Bourne now source wines from Australia, Chile, New Zealand, Argentina, California and South Africa as well as from the more traditional sources in Europe. In tandem with this growth in sourcing has been the appearance of new grape varietals; Pinot Grigio, Malbec, Pinotage, Chenin Blanc and Zinfandel.

There have also been a number of acquisitions of other wine businesses – in the mid-90's, Woodford Bourne purchased the wholesale business of Mitchell & Son in Dublin, while in 2001, the company added on Ecock Wine & Spirits Ltd. In 2004, the company achieved a long-held desire to expand into Northern Ireland with the purchase of the wholesale division of Direct Wine Shipments in Belfast.

Despite all the changes in the Irish wine market over the last 15 years, many of the companies relationships with key principals remain unchanged. Torres, Brown Brothers, Champagne Bollinger and Pasqua are just some of the names that continue to appear in the Woodford Bourne portfolio. An emphasis on fine and premium wines as well as a philosophy of working with quality, family-owned wineries has meant that the company continues to be one of the key wine importers in Ireland.

The market for table wines, fine and fortified wine has continued to grow in Ireland. Total wine sales have grown to an astonishing 7.6 million cases per year by 2004, with over 90% accounted for by table wines. This growth and opportunity has encouraged many other companies to enter the market. The substantial development of wine and spirit sales in supermarkets, and lately the resurgence of off-license sales as customers are choosing to consume the products in their own homes, has also influenced growth. The number one wine-supplying country to the Irish market by volume is now Australia with 23.2%, closely followed by Chile with 21.5%. France, once the dominant supplier to Ireland, now accounts for 18% of the market. Annual per capita wine consumption still remains one of the lowest in Europe at 15.3 litres with the UK at 20.1 litres and France at 48.5 litres.

A view of a section of the roof, showing the devastation caused by the extensive fire in the first floor of the Mardyke premises, in 1993. Following careful restoration, the Cork Corporation awarded the company two first prize awards. In 2001 the company won the award for the best restoration of an Historic Building followed by an award in 2003 for the best signage in the City.

Mary Brazier, Financial Director of The Mardyke, who worked with Woodford Bourne until 1988.

It would be a happy outcome if this book indicates how a family-run business played its part in developing the wines and spirits industry in Ireland, through its interaction with varying economic and social conditions over the span of 250 years in business. One thing is clear, the wines and spirits industry will continue to grow, responding to new and changing needs, new markets and the development of new ideas.

Barbucha's, one of the new bars in the Mardyke Leisure Complex.

mardyke

BARS | POOL | BOWLING | EVENTS

Epilogue on a Family Business

When the wholesale business was sold in 1988 the business of Woodford Bourne, when traced back to its oldest part, had been trading since 1750 – a span of 238 years. Allowing for an average working career of 30 years this covers a period of some 8 generations. At the time of the sale, the Nicholson family was in the process of transferring the management of the company to the 5th generation, some of whom continue to own and manage parts of the business to this day.

This longevity in a business is highly unusual. The survival of the business to the fourth generation of family is only achieved by some 5% of family businesses. While many business importing wines and spirits trace their roots back a significant distance, many as we have seen, found it difficult to adapt to the commercial reality of consumer markets, especially after the Second World War.

Of primary importance in the sustained success of Woodford Bourne was the commitment to the business by family and staff and the resultant pride in what the business was striving to achieve. The late nineteenth century saw innovation both in the grocery business and, perhaps more importantly, in the building of the Sheares Street warehouse and the installation of bottling machines. The attention to customer service and to product quality was to be the hallmark of Woodford Bourne throughout its history. Indeed it was the willingness of the company to take risks and invest in new products and channels of distribution, that enabled it to compete in the new commercial environment of the 1970s and early 1980s, as customer tastes became increasingly more diverse.

Another factor contributing to the success of the business, was the ability to form and sustain sound commercial relationships with a wide variety of suppliers, bottlers, customers, trade associations, bankers and the manufacturers of some of the products developed by the business. This ability to foster long term relationships has been one of the key strengths of all successful families in business and the companies which they own and manage.

Woodford Bourne never experienced any industrial or staff unrest throughout its history. Many staff remained with the company for the full duration of their working lives; this changed only towards the end of the company's history as some doubts crept in regarding the long term commitment of the family to the business. The element of trust is a further vital ingredient for longevity and is one which is evident in all successful family businesses. With trust comes commitment.

The concepts and thinking around the "ownership" of a family business are little explored. In the case of Woodford Bourne the careful stewardship of the capital of the business, especially in the early years, was of paramount importance. James Adams Nicholson had the foresight to invest in a new warehouse against a background of the economic recession and political unrest of the 1870s in Ireland. Board minutes over the following 40 years show his constant vigilance over dividend payouts and salary payments to the family: he recognised the importance of maintaining the profits in the business.

James Adams Nicholson also appreciated the ease of distraction with misguided investment in other commercial ventures external to the business. His experience of the collapse of the Munster Bank and thirty years later, the Britannia Motor Cab company provided concrete examples of the dangers of investing capital in unrelated and external businesses. In both cases Woodford Bourne lost scarce capital as the deliberations over the ongoing management of both issues took up valuable Board time and resources. The valuable lesson was the importance of focus on the main business; this was tested in the mid 1920s when the Board considered and turned down, the possible purchase of a distillery.

The consequent re-investment in the wholesale and retail business brought continuing profits. Woodford Bourne only lost money three in its history; once in 1924 following independence from Britain, in 1936 against a backdrop of the Great Depression and the loss of the Government contract to supply the British forces remaining in the Treaty port and finally in 1983 when economic conditions in Ireland, especially in the Cork region, affected performance and profitability. Continued profitability ensured adequate resources (lines of credit) for re-investment and sustainable relations with the shareholders.

From the mid 1880s onwards the ownership of the company was identified with one family. From the example and vision of James Adams Nicholson up to and including the entrepreneurial flair of David Nicholson, four generations of the family managed the company. Succession – often the *bete noir* of family companies – was achieved through primogeniture (the eldest son managed the business). The family also recognised the importance of policies to guide those family members who wanted to work in the business; these were written into the Minutes of the Board for clarity and emphasis.

A key element in the running of a family business is the realisation that the senior member cannot do everything himself and that the next generation is not necessarily prepared to take on the reins. As early as the 1920s the first non-family manager was appointed to the Board. As the business grew in the 1960s and 1970s more non-family managers were appointed to the Board, culminating with the appointment of Ken Daunt as Managing Director in 1980. A further point illustrating the trust the family put in others is their acceptance of outside help and advice apart from that routinely provided by the company auditors. The use of the I.P.C. demonstrated the willingness to share the problems and challenges of the company with qualified non-family professionals external to the company. This brought a new and fresh perspective to both the strengths of the company and the opportunities it faced, at a time when it was growing rapidly.

When, if at all, is the right time to sell a family company?. The sale of the wholesale wines and spirits businesses and some of the properties enabled the family to exit while maintaining the individual ownership of some of the remaining pubs, restaurants and employment businesses. These have grown and developed in the intervening 17 years since the sale. The continued ownership of the Woodford Bourne wines and spirits wholesale business would have required considerable investment in a difficult economic environment. This would have required the divestment of some of the properties to finance this investment, given the extortionate rate of interest on commercial loans prevalent at the time. The associated business risk, sale of property assets coupled with the desire of some of the family to exit, moved the family towards the difficult decision to sell.

Finally, what is the legacy of the 238 years of the business and the four generations of involvement by the one family? The company undoubtedly made a significant impact on the wines and spirits industry in Ireland. The sourcing of new wines from all over the world, coupled with a willingness to develop new products of its own, certainly contributed to the maturing of the wine market in Ireland. Many of the wines originally sourced by Woodford Bourne are still sold successfully in the wine market today under the Woodford Bourne name. A number of the other businesses remain in family control, being managed by the fifth generation. The process of the sale and handover of the company was achieved effectively and efficiently enabling all to continue with their individual projects while remaining justifiably proud of the achievements and success of Woodford Bourne.

This book is the story of how a family owned and run business played a significant role in the development of the wine and spirit industry in Ireland, against the canvas of the varying economic, social and political conditions over the span of its history. The story of Woodford Bourne has many valuable lessons and insights for the longevity of family companies. The lesson learnt by Woodford Bourne was that there was a constant need to keep abreast of the market, resulting from a rapidly changing commercial environment, led by the major drinks companies. A private family firm can find it almost impossible to find the resources to compete and can be left with the options to either merge and lose its identity, or sell in the hope and belief that its name will live on based on the reputation it handed over. This Woodford Bourne has achieved with pride. The wines and spirits industry will continue to grow, responding to changes, new markets and ideas. Family business, and the understanding of family business, will continue to play an important part in the commercial landscape in Ireland. The legacy of Woodford Bourne is that is has contributed to both.

Philip Mackeown

Cork , August 2005

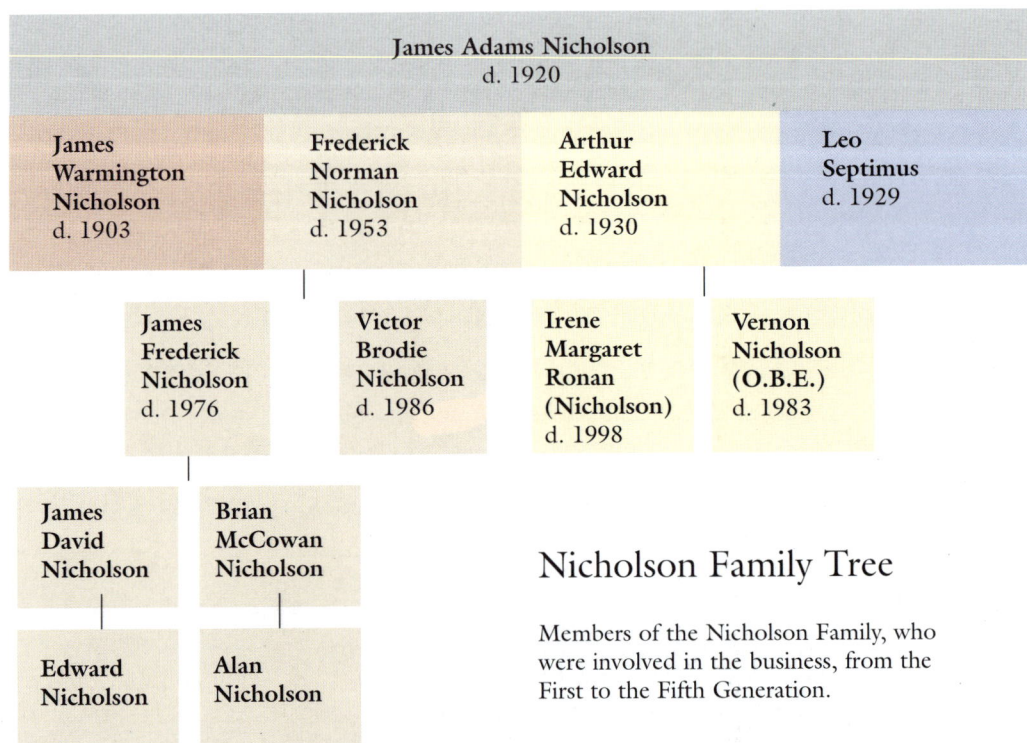

James Adams Nicholson d. 1920			
James Warmington Nicholson d. 1903	Frederick Norman Nicholson d. 1953	Arthur Edward Nicholson d. 1930	Leo Septimus d. 1929
	James Frederick Nicholson d. 1976	Victor Brodie Nicholson d. 1986	Irene Margaret Ronan (Nicholson) d. 1998	Vernon Nicholson (O.B.E.) d. 1983

James David Nicholson	Brian McCowan Nicholson
Edward Nicholson	Alan Nicholson

Nicholson Family Tree

Members of the Nicholson Family, who were involved in the business, from the First to the Fifth Generation.

About the Authors

David Nicholson

David Nicholson joined Woodford Bourne in 1954 after completing his undergraduate degree in Trinity College, Dublin, eventually succeeding his father as Managing Director of the business in 1969. He continued in this position until 1988 with the sale of the wholesale wine and spirits business, whereupon he gradually phased into retirement, handing over the retail business to his son Eddie. David is a keen sailor and a member of the Royal Cork Yacht Club, Kinsale Yacht Club and the Irish Cruising Club and is a former Commodore of the last two. Prior publications include the account of his cruising exploits over 50,000 sea miles in the Atlantic, Mediterranean and Baltic waters. David is married to Joan with four grown up children and lives in Monkstown, Co. Cork.

Philip Mackeown

A graduate of Trinity College Dublin, Philip worked for two years in London prior to joining his family wholesale business where he worked for 10 years in a number of operations roles, both in Ireland and Spain. Following the completion of an MBA with the Michael Smurfit School of Business in 2001, Philip has undertaken a number of consulting assignments and is a Visiting Lecturer to UCC where he lectures in the area of Family Business Management. Philip is married to Yvette and they live in Crosshaven, Co.Cork together with their four children.

Permissions

I would like to thank the following people and institutions for allowing us to reproduce material and photographs used in the book.

Woodford Bourne, Dublin; Michael Finnegan at the The Wine Promotion Board; Paul McCarthy at the Irish Examiner Archives; The Curator of the Cork Public Museum; Claire Taaffe at Business and Finance Magazine; The Editor of Checkout Magazine; Mrs Elizabeth Beattie, wife of the late artist R.D. Beattie; Ana Maria Borges of the Confraria do Vinho do Porto (Port Wine Brotherhood, Oporto, Portugal), and Noel Tymlin of Findlater Grants

Bibliography

Lawless Lee G. The Huguenot Settlements in Ireland. Longmans.

Cork Historical and Archaeological Society, *Two Famous Numismatists*.

Two Centuries of Progress Reminiscences of Fred N Nicholson c.late 1940's, early 1950's

Stratten and Stratten (1892) Dublin, *Cork and South of Ireland – a Literary, Commercial and Social Review Past and Present.* London.

Kennedy, K., Giblin T., McHugh D., (1988) *The Economic Development of Ireland in the Twentieth Century*, Routledge, London.

O'Hagan J.W. ed. (2000) *The Economy of Ireland: Policy and Performance of a European Region* (8th ed.) Gill and Macmillan, Dublin.

Whelehan T.P. *The Irish Wines of Bordeaux.*

Footnotes

Chapter 2

[1] (1895) Cork and South of Ireland: a Literary, Commercial and Social Review Past and Present. Page pp 153-154.

[2] Ibid Page 225.

[3] Ibid. Page 154.

Chapter 3

[1] Board Minutes 7 April, 1909.

[2] Memorandum and Articles of Association of Woodford, Bourne and Co. Limited.

[3] Board Minutes 5 May 1914.

[4] Board Minutes 5 December, 1913.

[5] Board Minutes 11 August, 1916.

[6] Board Minutes 5th May, 1918

Chapter 4

[1] Board Minutes 31 December, 1923.

[2] Board Minutes.

[3] Board Minutes 7 September, 1925.

[4] Board Minutes 4th January, 1932.

Chapter 5

[1] Board Minutes 4th August 1942.

Chapter 7

[1] Board Minutes 21st October, 1965.

Chapter 8

[1] Board Minutes 3rd November, 1970

[2] Board Minutes 2nd September, 1968.

Chapter 9

[1] Board Minutes 27th July, 1970.

Chapter 11

[1] Board Minutes 27th March, 1979.

Chapter 12

[1] Wine Development Board of Ireland factsheet.

[2] The figures for 2004 are based on official trade statistics, a Wine Development Board Country of Origin Survey (2004), and other trade sources.

COMPANY STAFF PHOTOS THROUGH THE AGES

Woodford Bourne Key Dates Timeline 1750 to 1900

1750 to 1824
Wine and Spirit Business founded by Peter Maziere in Falconers Lane

Products Importers and bottlers of Porter, Port, Marsala, Rum, Sherry

People Peter Maziere | Richard Sainthill joins as partner (1824)

1824 to 1860
Woodford and Co. set up in Patrick Street, Woodford Bourne and Co. (1850)
James Adam Nicholson manager of Woodford Bourne and Co (1860) | Famine in Ireland (1845 -1850)

Products General and Specialist grocers | Warrant to Supply the Naval Base and Barracks (1855)

People Woodford dies in 1845 | Bourne (manager) marries widow in 1850 | J A Nicholson (1860)

1860 to 1880
Assets of Maziere and Sainthill purchased by Woodford Bourne and Co (1869)
Nile Street Warehouse built in Cork (1873/5) | Global economic crisis from 1870s onwards

Products Registration of Brands (1870) – Whiskey, Port, Brandy, Sherry, etc.

People Richard Sainthill Dies (1869) | J.A Nicholson Managing Director (c.1865)

1880 to 1900
Appointment of London agent (1895) | Collapse of Munster Bank
Gas Engine to Paul Street entrance to Grocery Shop | Trademarks registered | Patrick Street store remodelled (1891)

Products Iris Whiskey exported to Britain | Whiskey sales to British forces

COMPANY STAFF PHOTOS THROUGH THE AGES

Woodford Bourne Key Dates Timeline 1900 to 1954

1900 to 1910

Grocery store opened in O'Connell Street, Limerick (1900) | Formation of Limited Company (1904)
Bottling in Bond Commences (1909)

People Directors Ord.Share: James Adams 1000 | Frederick Norman 600 | Arthur Edward 500 | Leo Septimus 400

1910 to 1920

Commencement of Grocery and Drink delivery business around Cork & Hinterland | Brittania Motor Cab Company Loan (1910)
50 Butts of Whiskey sent to Bond in Scotland, as insurance against political unrest | Bad Debts exposure | 1914 to 1918 War
Price Inflation | Post-War recession | War of Independence | Payment of £4000 to Lloyds for failure of Brittania Motor Cab
Company (1920)

Products Tea blending and Coffee roasting in Patrick Street store
Warrant to Supply Wine to Kings representative in Ireland (1911) | Whiskey Price inflation in 1917

People James Adams Nicholson dies (1920) | Frederick Norman Nicholson Managing Director (1920)

1920 to 1930

Loss of Government Contracts (1921) | Nile Street becomes Sheares St (1930) | Advertising in Cork Examiner and Evening Echo
Equity and ownership difficulties in the Company | Trading difficulties due to Civil unrest

Products Whiskey blending & bottling | Product Label development | Contract to supply Hospitals in the Irish Free State (1930)

People Victor Brodie Nicholson joins (1922) | James Frederick Nicholson joins (1929) as secretary | Staff of 17 and 4 Directors

1930 to 1945

Remodelling of Grocery and Wine premises in 65 Patrick Street (1932) | Ports lose British presence (1936) | War 1939 to 1945
Purchase of Oyster Tavern (1943)

Products Wholesale ~ Travelled Rounds, Guinness & Brown label | Retail ~ Sherry, Scotch, Rum, Port, Brandy, All House Brand
labels | WB appointed Munster distributors for White Horse Scotch Whiskey. | Whiskey Quotas

People W.T. Smye appointed first non-family Director | James Frederick Nicholson– Wine | Victor Brodie Nicholson – Grocery
Vernon Nicholson and Irene sell Ordinary Shares to existing Directors.

1945 to 1954

Closure of Limerick Shop(1946) | Brazenhead Bar and Grill opened (1950)

Products Development of Table wines | Shop ~ Tea and Coffee Blending, Sharwood, Barker and Dobson, Huntley and Palmer,
Fuller Cakes

People Frederick Norman Nicholson dies i(1953)| David Nicholson, BA BComm TCD joins (1954) | 20 Employees 1948)

COMPANY STAFF PHOTOS THROUGH THE AGES

Woodford Bourne Key Dates Timeline 1954 to 1978

1954 to 1960

Brazenhead Bar and Grill closed (1960) | Whittaker Report (1958)

Products Development of Retail laying down ~ fine Bordeaux wines also France, Germany, Italy, Spain imports.

1960 to 1970

Catering contract with Bunratty Castle | Proactive development of wine agencies
Agents for Export of Jameson Whiskey to the USA (1958) 5 Bottle Packs for Liners
Sponsorship of Oyster Festival | Development of Dublin market in late 1960's | Turners Cross Off Licence (1964)
Cash and Carry in Cork Warehouse (1966) | Bishopstown & Limerick Shops | Cash and Carry in Waterford (1967)
Ballintemple Shop (1968) | Central Staff Agency (1967) | Irish Vintners founded (1968) | Ireland joins the EC (1970)
Jamesons cease to supply bulk whiskey to trade

Products Festival of Wine (1964) tasting etc in warehouse indicated to the company the growing potential of the wine market.
Development of Europa Cyprus Sherries (1967) | Bottling line modernised in 1970

People Brian Nicholson joins (1961) | Ken Daunt joins (1964)
Gordon Hunter – Off Licence and Supermarket development in Dublin | David Nicholson MD (1969)

1970 to 1975

Join Irish Vintners (1970) - 24% share. C&C in Limerick(1971) | C&C in Dublin in Warehouse (1972)
C&C in Galway(1974) | Reardens Cellar Bar (1974) | Information flow on market and product developments.
Lost of cost advantage for local bottled wines. | Sales exceed £1.0 million (1972) | Purchase of Reardens Pub (1974)
High economic growth and stability.

Products Mirabeau Wines | Valpolicella, Bardolino, Soave - Pasqua (early 70's)
Beaujolais Nouveau race winners (1971) | Poteen Joint Venture (1971) Vermouth, Filapetti | Torres Agency (1975)
Bottling Guntrum wines

People Frank Donegan – Dublin (1972) | Terry Connolly – Buyer and Stock Controller (1973)
Jerry Cashman – Sales Controller (1975)

1975 to 1978

Wine Market share of c 18% - 2nd in market behind Gilbeys – by 1978.

Products Woodford Bourne Wine awards and golf promotion | Irish agent for Codorniu Cava (1976)
Taylors Port, Bollinger champagne | New World wines

People James Frederick Nicholson dies (1976)

COMPANY STAFF PHOTOS THROUGH THE AGES

Woodford Bourne Key Dates Timeline 1978 to 1988 et seq.

1978 to 1980
IPC Report #2 – Overtrading
Control difficulties in C&C – closures of Waterford, Limerick and Galway cash and carrys. Direct delivery to cut stocks.
Maguires Pennyfarthing Inn (1979) | Worsening economic environment | 18% Inflation
Products Royal Tara cream liqueur (1979) with Mitchelstown creamery 30% | Codorniu Award (1980)

1980 to 1985
Woodford Bourne leave Irish Vintners (1980) | Mandy's Cork (1980) | Mandy's Dublin (1982) Sold (1984)
Mardyke Snooker Club (1983) | Reardens Sold
Products Cease to sell any products not controlled by Woodford Bourne | Tauntons Cider – Dry Blackthorn (1985)
Royal Tara wins Gold Medal in Amsterdam (1982) | Sale of Royal Tara to Mitchelstown Creamery (1983)
People Ken Daunt MD (1980) | Hugh Duffy – Accountant | Frank Donergan – Marketing
Terry Connolly – Buyer and Operations | Nigel Leaming – Fast Food Consultant

1985 to 1988
IPC Report #3 (1986)
Products James Adams Vintners opens in Dublin (1985)
People Edward Nicholson joins company (1985) – Mardyke | Alan Nicholson joins company (1985) - CSA

1988 et seq
Sale of Company to Wardell Roberts (1988) | Patrick Street premises sold to McDonalds | Shops sold
DCC takes over Wardell Roberts (1990) and expands trade.
People Brian Nicholson takes over CSA | David Nicholson takes over Mardyke warehouse and pubs

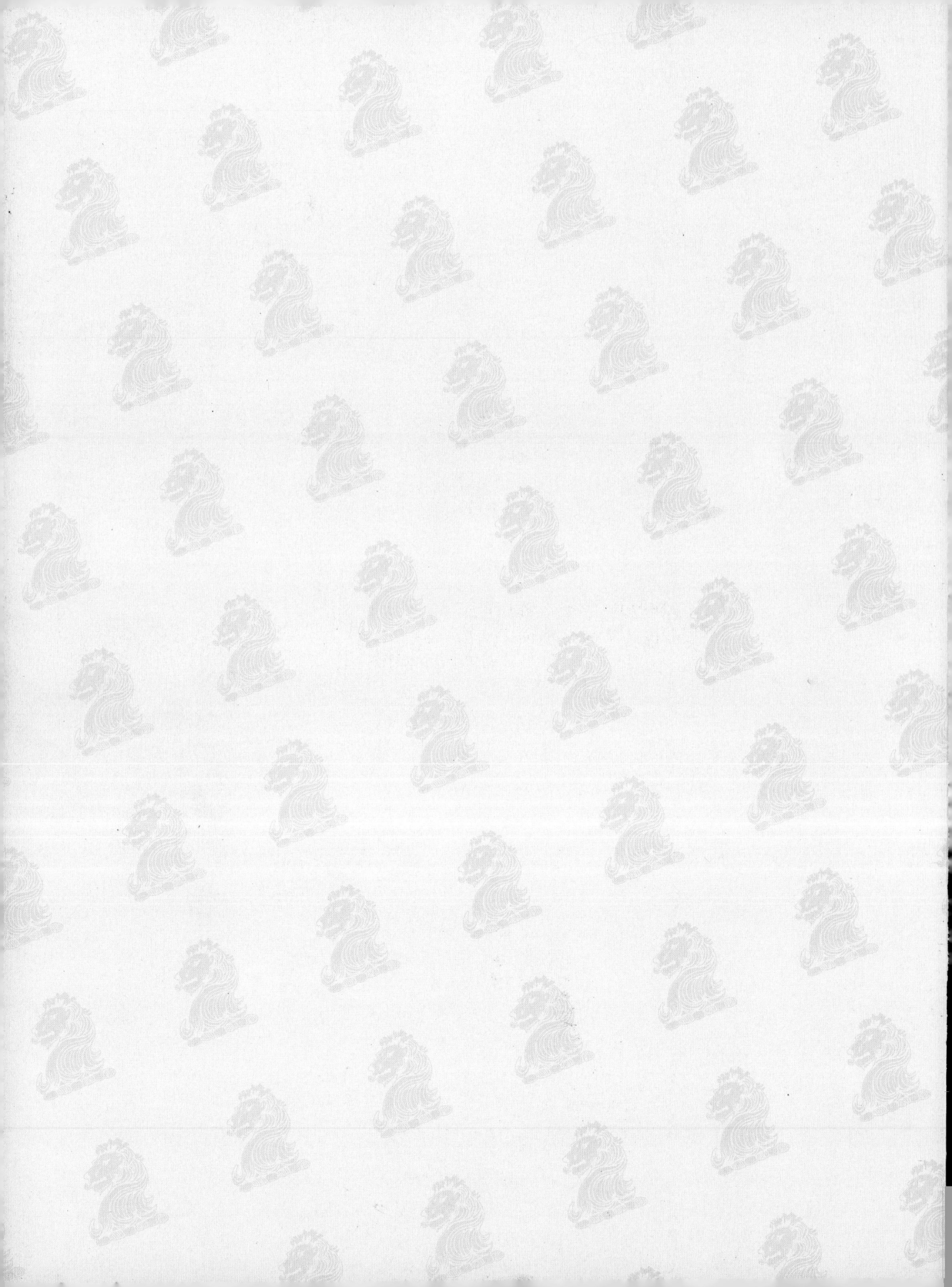